TOMORROW
IS BEAUTIFUL

To the Renew Team —

I pray that the following pages help to deepen your faith in the One who loves us all so much. Thank you for what you are doing in making such a difference around the world!

In Christ's love —
Jeff

Joshua 1:9

Jeff Jackson

ISBN 979-8-89112-045-7 (Paperback)
ISBN 979-8-89112-046-4 (Digital)

Copyright © 2023 Jeff Jackson
All rights reserved
First Edition

All rights reserved. No part of this publication may be reproduced, distributed, or transmitted in any form or by any means, including photocopying, recording, or other electronic or mechanical methods without the prior written permission of the publisher. For permission requests, solicit the publisher via the address below.

Covenant Books
11661 Hwy 707
Murrells Inlet, SC 29576
www.covenantbooks.com

INFORMATION PAGE

Cover photo- overlooking Chamo Lake, near Arba Minch, Ethiopia, taken by David Argabright

Unless otherwise noted, all Scripture taken from the New King James Version.

Copyright © 1982 by Thomas Nelson, Inc. Used by permission. All rights reserved.

In memory of

> Willson Aigner
> Larry Fox
> Lorn Taylor

Those who understood the call and did something about it.

> Precious in the sight of the Lord is the death of His saints.
> —Psalm 116:15

CONTENTS

Foreword ix
Introduction xi

Chapter 1:   In the Beginning 1
Chapter 2:   Island Hopping 6
Chapter 3:   An Unexpected Friendship 12
Chapter 4:   Try, Try Again 16
Chapter 5:   When You're Not Feeling It 20
Chapter 6:   How Did That Get in My Bag? 25
Chapter 7:   Earthquake 30
Chapter 8:   Night of the Hyena 34
Chapter 9:   Welcome Back, Boys 38
Chapter 10: You Can't Get There from Here 43
Chapter 11: Huambisa 48
Chapter 12: Hello, Patagonia 53
Chapter 13: The Uttermost 58
Chapter 14: The Torch 64
Chapter 15: The Day No One Will Forget 69
Chapter 16: Well, What Now? 74
Chapter 17: Just Take a Taxi 79
Chapter 18: The Land of Coconuts 84
Chapter 19: The Raid on Entebbe 89
Chapter 20: Where Did All the Witch Doctors Go? 93
Chapter 21: Into the Mouth of the Dragon 99
Chapter 22: Papers Please 103
Chapter 23: Of Snakes and Such 108
Chapter 24: The Road to Damascus 112
Chapter 25: Rice as Far as You Can See 117

Chapter 26: Stephen 122
Chapter 27: One Voice in the Night 126
Chapter 28: (   ) 130
Chapter 29: Moroccan Nights 135
Chapter 30: Where Did Dave Go? 140
Chapter 31: Pass the Yuca Please 145
Chapter 32: Enlighten Me 151

The Story Continues 157

FOREWORD

God radically changed my life during my first Work & Witness team to the Dominican Republic in 1982. God radically changed my ministry when Jeff Jackson joined a Virginia pastor's Work & Witness team I led to the Dominican Republic in 1999.

I know no one who has sacrificed more for Work & Witness teams and delivering JESUS Film equipment overseas than Jeff and Angie Jackson. You are about to have your world rocked by reading this incredible book about Jeff's journey of international volunteer mission service.

Jeff has seen God perform many miracles, and he unpacks the journeys so well in this book. I have been blessed to run with Jeff over the decades and have served with him on five continents since our first trip together. I always felt closer to Jesus when I served with Jeff. We have witnessed God close the eyes of customs agents when going through customs with JESUS Film equipment and move in the hearts of men and women in late-night church services and JESUS Film showings when we were exhausted after working all day in the hot sun.

In October 2013, while serving in Bangladesh, Jeff presented an especially powerful devotional that I will never forget. Angie's parents had recently passed away. However, she felt strongly that Jeff should go to Bangladesh with me and help lead this team. I will never forget the challenge Jeff presented. "Therefore, my brothers, stand firm. Always give yourselves fully to the work of the Lord, because you know that your labor in the Lord is not in vain" (1 Corinthians 15:58 NIV84). I can testify that Jeff and Angie have stood firm and given themselves fully to the work of the Lord.

JEFF JACKSON

Jeff and Angie's sacrifice and service are unmatched. It has been such a blessing for me and my family to serve with them. This book captures so many great memories, and once I started, I could not put it down. It is beautifully written, and I believe is a pleasing offering to God. Praise the Lord! I agree, *Tomorrow Is Beautiful*.

—David Argabright
Work & Witness team leader

Your ears shall hear a word behind you saying, "This is the way, walk in it," whenever you turn to the right hand or whenever you turn to the left.

—Isaiah 30:21

INTRODUCTION

Many times after I would be asked to speak or would share a story in a conversation, I would get the comment "You need to write a book" presented back to me. I just figured people were being nice. I never had any intention of writing anything and wouldn't even know how to approach such a venture.

There were other reasons why I would resist this effort. You'll see that some of the stories I'm about to share with you could be viewed as a bit sensitive and could jeopardize the safety of future overseas endeavors. This is also the reason I never got on social media. I never wanted some official in a foreign country to do a routine search on little old me while they were holding my passport in the back room of immigration…and I've been in a few.

But the biggest reason why I've resisted over the years is that I never wanted to gain any glory or attention that clearly doesn't belong to me. I've only been a willing passenger in the work that God Himself has orchestrated and continues to implement around the world today. He's the One we should focus on throughout the following pages. And He's the One Who has impressed upon me that, after many years, the time is now to share some of our stories together.

Dozens of you who are about to read this book will recognize some of the places and stories because you were there too. Please forgive me for not mentioning your names. For the sake of clarity and, in some cases, safety, it seemed best to keep the number of names in the stories to a minimum. I figure you know who you are, and more importantly, God does as well. I thank you all for saying yes to the call and being a part of His adventures. You're all heroes in my heart. Some names of cities in certain countries have also been left out for the protection of others who still might be there.

You will be introduced to a ministry tool called the JESUS Film and its effect globally. Questions that are often raised are, "Why do you have to personally take the JESUS Film equipment to other countries? Can't you just ship it there?" Reasonable questions that can be answered with, "It's illegal in many of these countries, and other countries are so corrupt that the equipment would never be delivered, or a payoff to release it would be double or triple the value of the equipment." That's why we take it.

You'll also be introduced to something called Work & Witness. It's a program through the Church of the Nazarene where a group of volunteers will travel overseas to help construct any structures like houses, churches, schools, etc. in communities in need. This has been a highly effective ministry over the years of combining faith with works and has changed the lives of thousands.

First of all, I want to thank you, the reader, for investing the time and effort to read this book. I hope you find it worthy of your investment. I also want to thank all those who have trusted me over the years whether it was domestically or on foreign soil. I sometimes question your sanity.

I also want to thank my wife, Angie, who has been a rock-solid support over the years in these adventures. I couldn't have gone anywhere if we weren't on the same page. This is rather ironic since the main issue she requested of me in our premarital counseling sessions way back in the day was to not travel for work and to be home. My reply then was, "You've got nothing to worry about. I'm not planning on going anywhere." I guess the Lord had other plans...but technically it hasn't been for work.

And most of all, I need to thank Jesus Christ for trusting me enough to partner with Him to help share His story with so many. I'll never know why He would choose someone who didn't say his first word until he was three (and hasn't said much since), to speak in front of crowds in so many different cultures for Him. But here we are.

I challenge you as you read on to see if God is still active in His pursuit to bring humanity into a personal relationship with Him, or is God just the God on the pages of a two-thousand-year-old book? I now invite you on some of the journeys He has taken me on over the years. I'll let you decide for yourself.

> For you will be His witness to all men of what you have seen and heard. And now why are you waiting?
> —Acts 22:15–16A

Do all the good you can.
By all the means you can.
In all the ways you can.
In all the places you can.
At all the times you can.
To all the people you can.
As long as ever you can.

—John Wesley

CHAPTER 1

IN THE BEGINNING

Have you ever felt like you're not quite sure what you're doing here or what your purpose is? Life seems to be going on well enough, but something deep inside is just off, and you're not sure what it is or what to do about it. Most of the time it's "out of mind" because of the busyness of life, and we click off the days, weeks, and months not focusing much on it, until we have a moment to stop and think.

That's where I was and I'm sure I'm not alone with those thoughts. My brother Jim and I grew up working construction with our dad. He did mostly commercial construction and traveled all over east of the Mississippi river for his jobs. We would join up with him from time to time when he was on the east coast and gained a knowledge of construction and work ethic.

The last two years of my high school career were spent in Washington, DC. My mom ran three boarding houses for international students. We would have up to forty-five people there at a time, and it opened my eyes a bit to cultures from all over the world. It was quite an experience, but I didn't think that much about it until years later.

When I went off to college, I was a bit of a goofball and had a tendency to pull some pranks on fellow students and even faculty from time to time. I was once coerced into confessing to an incident that I was involved with in my early years. Instead of repenting of my ways, I vowed to never get caught again and doubled down in my rogue activities throughout the rest of my college career...and held true to that vow by never getting caught again. I am more than thankful that the Lord's grace has been sufficient to bury all that.

I did get decent grades in college and double majored in history and business administration with aspirations to go on to law school somewhere. Jim had already graduated and gone on to get his master's in psychology. So armed with our degrees of higher education, when the opportunity came up, we naturally went right back into construction. I put my law school dreams on the back burner, and Jim put his master's degree on the shelf, and we started a residential framing company with Jim's brother-in-law Mike, in the South Shore area of eastern Massachusetts.

We were all married, and life was rolling along. Jim and I were beginning to grow our families, and the opportunity came up to move to the Chesapeake Bay area of Virginia and start building there. Mike stayed in Plymouth, Massachusetts, with his wife, Debi, and Jim and I made the move with our families and jumped right into building waterfront custom homes in the White Stone area of Virginia. White Stone is a very rural area, and we thought it would be great to raise our families there together.

Jim and his wife, Julie, had three sons, and Angie and I had three daughters. Life continued to click by. Rural life was great, but we didn't have a Nazarene church close by. That was important to us, so we would load up the families every Sunday and travel forty-five to fifty minutes to attend a small Nazarene church in the town of

West Point, Virginia. We did this for ten years. Life continued to click by.

It was around this time that talk was starting about planting a Nazarene church in the White Stone area. There were ten in our two families, and Angie's parents had recently moved to the area, and that made twelve. The problem was that the church in West Point ran thirty-six to forty people on a good Sunday, and that included the twelve of us.

I give a lot of credit to that West Point pastor to be willing to let a third of his congregation go for a possibility to multiply the Kingdom. Prayer, details, and planning were done on how this was going to work. Then our district superintendent, Rev. Charles Thompson, who was in charge of all the Nazarene churches in Virginia, wanted to have a meeting with me and my brother. I felt like I was going back to the dean's office.

He encouraged us and told us that we could do this with God's help and a faithful plan. (Years later, he would confess to me that he had some serious doubts about the whole White Stone endeavor.) And then at the end of the meeting, he said, "The only way we can do this is if one of you two agree to become the pastor." Jim and I just looked at each other in silence. Maybe that's when Reverend Thompson started to have his doubts. I'm not sure.

I never felt the call to be a pastor. In fact, I hated public speaking. The thought of standing in front of a crowd to address them would nauseate me. Jim and I agreed to work together on it. He would do the preaching, and I would do the visitations and other behind the scenes work. But for some reason, I still felt the need to go through the educational process to become ordained, although I wasn't sure why.

Jim and I both went back to school from home through a directed studies program at a Bible college to earn an equivalent of a four-year religion degree toward ordination. I felt like God was paying me back for the pranks I pulled on all those religion major students back in college. Life just got more exciting but was still clicking away.

The Lord blessed our efforts, and our little group of twelve soon grew close to a hundred. He also blessed the little church in West Point as they rebounded right away in attendance after losing us and began running around forty again. Sometimes it's best not to know what you're doing or what you're getting involved in. The White Stone church was growing, and God was doing it.

Jim and I had given up building homes, although I was still doing small projects of my own. And though life was busy with the church and family and schooling, that old feeling of what's my purpose was still gnawing at me. During this time, I was reading all kinds of material. Of course, I was reading my course of study books, but I was also reading a lot of religious magazines as well.

I came across an article that talked about a film that was being used in many different places around the world. It was put out by an organization called Campus Crusade for Christ. The film was taken completely from the Gospel of Luke and told the story of Jesus. It was called *The JESUS Film*. The fascinating detail was that this movie was being translated into the different languages where it was being shown, and thousands would hear Jesus and the Gospel spoken in their own language and then respond to the invitation to accept Jesus as their Savior.

I thought that was fantastic. What a great idea. But then in the following days, I couldn't stop thinking about it. I would go about my busy schedule day by day, and the thought of this film on foreign lands would keep coming back to me. But what could I do about it? There's already an organization handling the situation, and my plate is full here in White Stone.

A few weeks later, we were having our men's Bible study, and one of the guys came in late. Before he sat down, he said, "Hey, did you guys hear that the Nazarene church has partnered with Campus Crusade in the JESUS Film ministry?" Most of the guys looked at him sideways and had no idea what he was talking about. But something in me locked into place. I can't explain it. It was like opening a window shade and having the noonday sun hit you directly in the face. I couldn't wait for that Bible study to be over to try to get more details about it. My friend didn't have much more than that, so I went searching on my own.

I found out that Campus Crusade had shown the film to most of the major urban centers of the world and were looking for some Christian organization that could help them get it into more rural parts of the world. The Nazarene church had missions in its DNA when it started in the early 1900s and was a perfect fit for this project due to their extensive and organized missions network around the world.

I had no idea what to do; I just knew I had to get involved somehow. Jim was firmly established as the senior pastor by this time, and we had enough devoted members to help out in different duties around the church. But could God really use some no-name carpenter, former college pranking goofball, who doesn't like to speak in public, with only a little experience with foreigners, and had only traveled as far as Canada one time to go skiing? I would have to agree with old Reverend Thompson: "I have some serious doubts about the whole endeavor."

> For I know the thoughts that I think toward you, says the Lord, thoughts of peace and not of evil, to give you a future and a hope.
> —Jeremiah 29:11

CHAPTER 2

Island Hopping

I did a little research and found a missionary in the Philippines who agreed to take on some help in training some brand-new JESUS Film teams on different islands of that beautiful country. I didn't know what I was doing at the time, but I had a travel agent book my trip to Manila. After flying to Detroit, I loaded myself on the next plane for that long direct flight to Manila. Little did I know what it felt like to fly for about seventeen straight hours in one seat. After about eight hours, it really doesn't matter a whole lot. From that point on, it's all a kick in the teeth.

When I finally arrived late at night and what felt like three days later, I had to find my way outside the airport and hope my ride was there to get me. They didn't allow any visitors inside the terminal at that time. As I walked out the doors, the hot humid air engulfed me along with about a thousand Filipinos who blocked my way out toward the parking area. I bumped my way through the crowd looking for a man named Bob. A man I had never met or seen before. He spotted me first. I guess I must have stood out somehow.

Soon we were on our way through the Manila traffic and back to his place. I was going to be Bob's assistant for the next three weeks or so. The plan was to travel during the week to different main islands that make up the Philippines to train these new JESUS Film teams and try to make it back to Manila by the weekends before we would head out again the next week.

After a day of jet-lagged rest, which was more awake than asleep, Bob and I went to meet our local district superintendent who was in charge of all the Nazarene churches in the Philippines and was going to be our traveling companion on our adventures. As we were sitting in his living room, he came walking in with a bowl full of large eggs still in their shells. Everyone else who was there took one, so I figured I better take one too.

They called it balut. I had never heard of it before. I sat there and watched the others in the room to learn some kind of technique in how to eat what I assumed to be a hard-boiled egg the proper way. It didn't take me long to realize that this was no hard-boiled egg. Balut is an egg that has been incubated for a number of days before it is taken and steamed for a while and then handed to its consumer. So it's not quite a chick, and it's definitely not quite an egg. Ours happened to be from the duck variety.

I gently took off the top part of the shell and slurped and drank and chewed my way through this edible gift from my first host overseas. I don't normally drink sodas, but I was sure glad to have an open Coke sitting within arm's reach. As I finished up my snack, our host's wife walked by me, leaned over to me, and said, "I don't know why he eats those, I think they're disgusting." I just smiled. I found out later that eating balut is apparently good luck for traveling. I think I'd like to take my chances next time.

Our first trip was to be to the island of Mindoro. We left early in the morning so we could reach the ferry to get off the island of

Luzon and travel south to Mindoro. As we approached the ferry, there was a huge line of vehicles being inspected before being allowed onto the ferry. Manila has a high car theft rate, and inspectors check the vehicle numbers (VIN) to make sure they're not stolen and headed to another island to a chop shop and sold for parts. We were getting nowhere fast, and it looked like we were in danger of not making the ferry. Then our driver got out and approached one of the inspectors and apparently told him that Bob and I were Nazarene priests.

He came back to the car and looked at Bob and me sitting in the back seat and waved us through to the ferry and past everyone without checking any numbers on our vehicle at all. That's when I heard about a popular and powerful cult in the Philippines that's called the church of the Black Nazarene. It has nothing to do with the Church of the Nazarene that we were representing, but the inspector assumed we were officials with this other organization and opened a door for us to keep on schedule.

Mindoro had been recently hit by a strong typhoon, and the people were beginning to recover. A lot of food staples, like rice, had been shipped there to a local church, and once we arrived, we happen to be there to help distribute the items to the whole local village and area. That night, we had a service in the local Nazarene church, or what was left of it. Only the walls were left standing, and we worshipped under the starry skies.

I'll never forget when the people started singing together that worship tune "Give Thanks." To hear them all, who had almost been wiped out by a natural disaster singing the words, "Let the poor say I am rich, let the weak say I am strong, because of what the Lord has done for me," gathered in a roofless church was quite an experience. Every time I've heard that song since, I'm taken back to that night. I was able to share a message with them that night and tried to encourage them, but they had already encouraged me.

The next day, we met our new JESUS Film team for Mindoro. Most of these teams are made up of three to four men who are dedicated to traveling from village to village and set up and show the film publicly. They then follow up with those who accept Christ and help disciple them with basic Christian principles. Then they either get them into an existing church or start a church of new believers that an existing pastor can circuit ride to and minister to them. These teams work hard and sacrifice so much.

In this first training, I was basically being trained as well. We went over how to operate the equipment, the best strategy to get people to come out and watch the film, and how to follow up with those who came. The Philippine people are a warm and loving people who love community get-togethers. They also love basketball, and almost every village had an outdoor basketball court in the middle of it. This is where we would set up to show the film.

As people would show up, they were asked to fill out a small slip of paper with their name and address on it so they would have a chance to win a prize during the movie. When one of the four reels would have to be changed, a name would be called out during the quick break, and some lucky attendee would win an umbrella or other small prize. This was always communal fun and also gave us a bucket of names and addresses of everyone who was at the showing.

The next day, team members would go door to door armed with names and addresses to thank the people for coming out to the film showing and talk with them if they wanted to. We discovered that many people accepted the Lord in these follow-up encounters who wouldn't come forward during the public film showing. These strategies worked extremely well.

We stayed a few days in Mindoro before heading back to Manila. Our next trip was to the island of Cebu, which required an overnight ferry ride to reach. We trained our second team there and were joined by others who were potential future JESUS Film team members. After another trip back to Manila for the weekend, we set out for our last assignment on the big island called Mindanao. We flew to this one.

When we arrived, our district superintendent was there to pick us up. Mindanao had a different dynamic to it. Because of its location in the deep south, it was positioned close to Indonesia. Indonesia is the largest Muslim country in the world. Because of this, there were a lot of Muslims in Mindanao, and some terrorist activities had taken place there as well.

After our training of this new team, it was decided not to show the film on a basketball court but somewhere that would attract a bigger crowd. We decided to show it outside of a very busy bus station just outside the city of Cagayan de Oro. It just happened to be the site of a terrorist bus bombing just two weeks before we got there. It was a chance to bring the Gospel to a place that had recently been devastated.

We were right. It attracted a huge crowd. I watched the crowd for a variety of reasons, but I noticed men who were supposed to be unloading trucks slow way down in their movements and eventually sit on their cargo to watch and listen to Jesus talk to them in their own language. This night was a huge success as many came forward to accept Jesus. I was hooked on this ministry.

The next day before we wrapped up to leave back for Manila, Bob and I found ourselves in a small fishing village for another meal with the locals. For three weeks, I had been traveling around this beautiful country and eating many variations of their local cuisine. And here I found myself one more time at a table set for about twenty and loaded with different seafood and local favorites.

Bob and I were the only foreigners at the table. As we ate and fellowshipped together, the district superintendent said to the others there, "Hey, you guys remember those volunteers who came over here and only ate pancakes that they made themselves?" The whole table laughed out loud and said, "Yes!" Bob told me later about some young volunteers who had helped out over there but refused to eat anything that was given to them. They would set up their own griddle at meal times and proceed to make and eat their own pancakes. They did this for two weeks straight.

I couldn't tell you their names, but neither could the Filipinos. They only remembered them for eating pancakes. Perhaps the balut on the first night was a test. I didn't ask. I didn't need to at this point. The superintendent was comfortable enough to say something humorous about some foreigners with two foreigners sitting right at the table because he didn't look at Bob and me as foreigners anymore. He had accepted us as brothers. I figured if I ever went anywhere else in the world, I never wanted to be remembered as a nameless foreigner who ate pancakes but as a brother working together for the Kingdom of God.

> Whatever city you enter, and they receive you, eat such things as are set before you.
> —Luke 10:8

CHAPTER 3

AN UNEXPECTED FRIENDSHIP

Not long after returning from the Philippines, a powerful hurricane ripped through the Caribbean. It devastated the eastern part of the Dominican Republic. Jim and I were invited by Reverend Thompson to attend a pastor's retreat for the Virginia district pastors. While there, it was announced that the Virginia district pastors were forming a team of volunteers to go to the Dominican Republic to help the people rebuild. The team was to be led by a layman who had a lot of experience with volunteer teams like this. His name was Dave Argabright.

The Church of the Nazarene has a program called Work & Witness. This is where a group of volunteers will raise project material funds for a particular need and then travel to that area of the world to voluntarily help with the construction of that project. It has been highly successful, and Dave had been a part of it since the 1980s.

Reverend Thompson approached me privately and asked if I had any interest in going and being a part of this Dominican Republic project. I told him I would have to think about it. Little did I know that he had already asked Dave if he "could work with a guy like Jeff Jackson?" Dave didn't know me from Adam, so his reply was, "Well, as long as he works, I guess I can." Dave would tell me later that he thought to himself, *I can get along with about anybody, but who in the world is Jeff Jackson that Reverend Thompson needed to say this*? To this day, neither one of us knew what Reverend Thompson meant by that comment.

I still have a bit of a complex from it today. But looking back now, I could see what the Lord was doing and how He used a listening servant named Reverend Thompson to set it all up. I eventually signed up with about a dozen other pastors from the retreat. I was introduced to Dave, and I'm sure he was trying to size me up from the recent comments made to him that I didn't know anything about.

The eastern part of the Dominican Republic is made up of a lot of sugar cane fields. Large sugar companies control this industry and have low-wage labor work the crops for them. Almost all of these workers are immigrants who have come over from next door Haiti. These Haitians not only work the cane fields for these companies but also live out there in small company-built villages called batays.

It wasn't unusual to see one building in the batay with a white flag flying over it. This would let the people know where the voodoo priest resided. They could have a major influence among the Haitians. The people worked long hard hours in the cane fields. The pay was meager, and the existence was humble, but the people were happy to have work.

You can imagine the devastation a strong hurricane could bring to an area like this. The companies would take care of rebuilding the housing, but other important structures, like the local wooden churches, had also been wiped out. Our task was to help rebuild the churches. And we would rebuild them with cement blocks instead of wood. Not only would this make a nicer building, but it would also give the local community a stronger structure to shelter in for protection from future hurricanes that would eventually come to the Caribbean island.

This was my first time traveling with a group. It was a whole new dynamic. We flew to Santo Domingo and the traveled east to a city called La Romana. We were to lodge there in a large upper room over this city's church. Bunkbeds lined the two outside walls, and we settled in. I had an upper bunk, and Reverend Thompson took the lower portion of the same bunk. Thinking about it now, I don't know if that was just the way it worked out, or if he was trying to keep an eye on me. Either way, I have never been with a group of men who snored more than this one. They still hold the record today. You would think as much as pastors talk while they're awake, they would need to store up some silence at night. Man, was I mistaken. That's when I learned to always bring earplugs to the party, just in case.

Despite the lack of sleep at night, the project started out smoothly. A lot of blocks were being laid, and many friendships with the local people were starting to be established. Having a construction background and looking at how organized the whole event was, I could tell a lot of behind-the-scenes preparation had taken place to pull something like this off. That responsibility would have fallen mostly on Dave's shoulders and the field leaders.

On the weekend, we had the opportunity to worship with the people we had been working with during the week. The services were fantastic. As we finished up this first project, it was nice to see the bones of a new church standing there and know that it would be well used. This Work & Witness stuff seemed to be right up my alley. The Lord knew it, and I think Reverend Thompson knew it too. It was also nice to offset any buildings that had a white flag flying over it with a structure dedicated to the positive use of influencing the people with the Gospel of Jesus Christ.

Of all the positives that I took away with me on this Work & Witness trip, one of the biggest was a friendship that was beginning to be established with Dave. As the work days went on and the evening conversations took place, we got to know the hearts of each other. Of course, he still might have just been trying to figure me out based on Reverend Thompson's previous comments about me. I guess I passed. Our personalities were different but complimented each other, and we had the same passion for reaching the world for Christ by any means possible. Neither one of us had any idea at that time what the Lord had planned for the future.

This trip was just one of quite a few that were needed in this part of the Dominican Republic to get things halfway back to normal. I was on most of them, and so was Dave. But the Dominican Republic wasn't the only place needing structures built. There were needs all over the world. With the recent partnership that was established with the JESUS Film ministry, the opportunity to marry these two ministries in the future was taking place. I felt like the Lord had given me another brother to work alongside to get the Gospel out. But neither of us knew just how far the Lord would take us.

> For whoever does the will of God is my brother and sister and mother.
> —Mark 3:35

CHAPTER 4

Try, Try Again

Eventually Dave and I had gotten ourselves into being volunteer Work & Witness coordinators for the Horn of Africa. One of our main duties was to get physical structures built to help with the exploding church growth there. The church in Ethiopia was growing so fast that there was no way to keep up with building churches, so the plan was to build training centers strategically placed around the country. Pastoral leaders from rural areas would travel to these centers for training and teaching with the goal of going back to their rural areas and train and teach other leaders what they had recently learned. This leadership multiplication strategy worked well for a church that was in danger of becoming a mile wide and an inch deep spiritually.

One of the sites decided on to build one of these training centers was Arba Minch. Located in Southern Ethiopia, Arba Minch is one of the last metropolitan areas (and I use the term loosely) heading south toward Kenya. After Arba Minch is where many of the last remote tribes of Ethiopia dwell. The training center was to be a two-story building, so we planned to have two separate Work & Witness groups of guys come over and to each construct a story.

As the first group was laying block and doing their thing, the local JESUS Film team invited us to go with them in the evening to show the film in a village not too far away. To be a part of a JESUS Film showing was always an experience, and since the guys didn't have any plans, we cleaned up after work and piled into two vehicles and headed out into the night. Now before a JESUS Film team would go into a village to set up and show the film, they would always go there a day or so in advance and ask permission from the local chief or elder who was in charge. This would avoid any sort of offense or misunderstanding. Our team had secured the OK, and we looked forward to sharing the Gospel in their own language.

We drove on through the African night for about forty-five minutes when we finally made a left off the main road and onto a very rough dirt road. After a mile and a half of having our internal organs rearranged, we came into a clearing and parked. You could see huts spread out in the surrounding forest, but with no electricity, you couldn't tell how many there were or how big the village actually was.

We began to unload and set up the JESUS Film equipment, and people began to come out with curiosity to see what was going on. Once we had the outdoor screen erected, the projector on its stand, and the sound system hooked up and ready to go, the crowd had swelled to two hundred to three hundred curious onlookers. That's when we noticed one of the JESUS Film team members in a serious discussion with someone from the village. When they finished, our team member came over to us and informed us to start packing up the equipment. He said that the elder who gave us permission to show the film was away, and this gentleman was second in charge and that there was no way he was going to let us show a film about Jesus in his village. You gotta love politics.

The problem was that this current gentleman never made an announcement to the hundreds of anticipating villagers but turned and disappeared into the African night. With each piece of equipment taken down and packed up, you could sense the mood of the crowd beginning to change. From confusion to disappointment to anger, they didn't know why we would come out to them and get their hopes up only to pack up and leave. That's when the first rocks started flying.

It wasn't the first or last time that I had rocks thrown at me, but never from a crowd this big. My first thought was, *This could get ugly*. We told the guys to get in the vehicles *now* as we were practically throwing the equipment into the open back doors. The last few pieces came in with several handfuls of gravel from the angry mob. We slammed the doors and started moving before the crowd could surround the vehicles. As we drove out of the clearing, I was waiting for the side windows to blow out from the peppering we were taking, but they held.

Once we got back on the main road, we stopped to make sure everyone and everything was OK. That's when we noticed we were missing one of the guys. The good news was that he was an Ethiopian and had a better chance of blending in. The bad news was that someone was going to have to go back and get him. Our field director Howie, Dave, and I said we'd go, and we started back down that dark road toward the village. Praise the Lord our friend had already started walking out of the village, and we spotted him and picked him up before we went all the way back to that clearing. The team was happy things didn't get out of hand, but it showed us just how much of a dark spiritual stronghold still grips so much of the world today. That first team of guys finished up their part of the Arba Minch Center and had some stories to tell as well.

Several weeks later, the second team of guys arrived to do the next level of the center. One of the members, named Paul, from this new team was from my home church. Paul was a veteran of many Work & Witness trips as most of the guys who were there had been. While we worked, I happened to share with Paul about our incident in that village with the previous team. He soaked it up.

This new team of workers was rocking and laying block when the JESUS Film team came by one of the days and asked if we wanted to go with them to a showing that night. I thought to myself, *Surely it can't be as bad as last time. The Lord wouldn't let that happen to us again in another village.* So we said, "Sure," and cleaned up after work and headed out of Arba Minch and into the African night.

Paul was sitting next to me in our vehicle. As we drove along, I noticed we had headed out of town in the same direction as we did the first time. I just figured we were going to another village north of town. After about forty-five minutes, we began to slow down and took a left off the main road and onto a very rough dirt road that seemed eerily familiar. That's when I leaned over to Paul and whispered to him, "I think we're going back to that same village that just tried to kill us a few weeks ago." Paul was silent for a moment with his eyes as big as saucers. Now Paul was soaking this up.

Paul leaned over to me and whispered, "Should we tell the others?"

I said, "No, not yet…let's see how it goes." We pulled into the village clearing and parked. We started pulling out and setting up the equipment as a crowd began to gather. I must admit that I kept my head on a swivel as hundreds gathered again. This time the main village elder was present, and there were no incidents.

As the film played, my eyes caught a very short older woman with a big bundle of sticks on her back just standing there, hunched over as she stared at the lit screen, and listened to Jesus talking in her own language. She watched the whole film as did hundreds of others. When an invitation was given to accept Jesus, dozens came forward and prayed. I was stunned at the different spirit that had taken over this village. Just a few short weeks before, they would've had our heads if they could, but now a transformation had begun because of a Man Who spoke their language and went to the cross for them.

> Behold I will do a new thing, now it will spring forth; Shall you not know it? I will even make a road in the wilderness and rivers in the desert.
> —Isaiah 43:19

CHAPTER 5

WHEN YOU'RE NOT FEELING IT

We had traveled to the Amazon jungle plenty of times by this point and had always enjoyed working with Dr. Larry Garman and whatever Work & Witness projects he had going on. You knew when you went to work with Doc that things would be organized, and you were expecting to be worn out by the end of the trip.

If there was ever a couple that epitomized what being a missionary was, it was Larry and Addie Garman. They had spent over forty years in the Peruvian Amazon jungle ministering to a tribe called the Aguaruna. They had established hundreds of churches, a school, a clinic, etc. while bringing thousands to the Lord. They also addressed the medical needs of the people all while raising their own family in this harsh environment. They were tireless and a perfect example of Christlikeness and humility. So when you went to work with them, you better be ready to work and to minister.

Most of the trips we took with Doc were a bit on the rustic side (to say the least), and due to the potential danger, our teams were almost always made up of men. We would typically leave the mission station on the Marañón River in a couple of open johnboats and then travel down the river to other rivers until we reached the first Aguaruna village where we would work and stay.

It was always a village in need of a church structure, and the well-seasoned small group of guys that would go on these adventures knew the drill. We could typically construct a wooden church in about a day and a half complete with a metal roof. Granted these were not Solomon's Temple, but they were a closed-in structure of about twenty by forty feet. That would be more than adequate in these primitive conditions. We would usually have a team of six to ten guys who would venture into the Peruvian jungle for these projects.

You could expect the days to be hot and the nights to be cool, and it didn't take long for the conditions to start wearing you out. Since we could build one of these churches in a day and a half, Doc would prepare for us to construct three of them in three different villages during our stays with him. Once we did four, but that's a story for later on. Our group was joined by a couple of local Peruvians who were from the mission station and the local district superintendent who oversaw all the churches in this part of the jungle. His name was Canisio.

We loaded up the two boats with our gear and our smiles and began to head out from the mission station and down the Marañón River. It took us several hours to reach the first village. What a welcome we received! It seemed like the whole village was on the bank of the river when we pulled up. They were so happy we were there to work in their village. We unloaded the boats and strung up our mosquito nets over our bamboo beds in the hut we would call home for the next two nights. We then began to get to work in laying out the new church building.

The villagers were so excited, like most of them are when we would arrive, they announced that they wanted to have a church service with us that night after dinner. Those services would always be something to experience. There was no electricity, so they would light candles, and the whole village would turn out for it. Many times the local pastor would ask if anyone would want to give a testimony or praise. Again it seemed like the whole village would line up one by one to thank God for us or the new church building or just the goodness of God in their lives. You can imagine that between all that and all the translations, these services could last well into the night. This first service was no exception.

The next day, we rock and rolled on the building and finished it in the afternoon. There wasn't enough daylight left to travel to the second village so we were there for one more night. As we were cleaning up and getting ready for dinner, we were told that the village wanted to have another service that night. We were a bit tired but had no other plans, so we again attended a service that went well into another candlelit night.

The next morning, we packed up our gear, loaded up our boats, said our goodbyes, and headed toward the next village. When we pulled up to the river bank of this village, it seemed to be a repeat of the first village with the whole population waiting to greet us. You couldn't blame them for their excitement. They didn't get many visitors to their village.

Once we got settled in and worked for a while, the local pastor came up to us and proclaimed, "We are so glad you are here. We want to have a church service tonight to praise the Lord and celebrate." And we did. Another line of testimonies, more songs sung, lengthy translations, and more candles burned well into the night. The next day, we mustered enough energy to finish the building, and the villagers were so excited, they wanted to say thank you by having a service in it that night…with us. It was another late one.

We left early the next morning because we were running out of overall days on our trip, and we still had one more village to go to. We figured if we could get to the last village early enough, we could get the majority of it built in one day and let the villagers finish up the odds and ends on it so we could start our long trek back out of the jungle. You can imagine by this point, we were all exhausted.

When we arrived at the third village, there was another large welcoming committee of beautiful smiling faces. I waited for the announcement of another service, but it didn't come as we set up in our hut and then began to work. We were focused on getting this last church up, and all the guys gave all they had left for the effort. As tired as we were, we worked until dark, but we got it done.

We tried to clean up as best we could in the dark, but none of us felt like it. We were totally spent. They announced to us that dinner would be in twenty minutes or so. I didn't even know what time it was. We were all looking forward to eating and collapsing in our hut.

As we sat there at dinner, staring blankly into our bowls of local cuisine, the local pastor came in and announced that a church service was to start in about twenty minutes, and the villagers wanted us there to celebrate and to thank us. I saw every single head around our dinner circle drop, including Canisio and Doc. I thought we would be lucky if we mustered enough strength to get to our hut after dinner to lie down. By the reactions around the table, I was not alone in that thought.

The last thing we wanted to do was to go to another lengthy service. Apparently, they had asked Doc to give the message this night because I saw him immediately pull out his pocket New Testament and began to thumb through it looking for a passage to preach on. Then Doc said, "Listen, guys, if we can just have a couple of testimonies from you guys, I won't have to preach. We can keep it short, and we can get out of there at a reasonable hour." I looked around the silent table, and everyone's head was still down. I don't think any of us had the strength to get up from the table let alone give a testimony. There was no response to Doc's request.

Somehow we dragged ourselves to that brand-new church in the dark. They already had benches in it, and the candles were lit. The whole village had shown up and filled the place. Since Canisio was in charge of overseeing this church, he got up to say a few words to the people. Then Doc got up and asked us as a group to see if we would be willing to get up and sing a song. That was normal for us at some point on a trip. We would normally sing either "This Is My

Story" or "There's Power in the Blood." It was never pretty, but those were two songs we all knew.

One of the Peruvians who had come with us from the mission station had brought a guitar, so we dragged ourselves up front and started to sing. As we were up singing, I looked at the front row. There was Canisio, already sound asleep, and next to him was Doc still thumbing through his pocket New Testament with his flashlight, still looking for a passage to speak on. I thought, *Wow, none of us are feeling it, not even the district superintendent or a forty-year veteran missionary.* We finished our song and sat back down.

Doc stood up with a translator next to him and in English said again, "Hey, guys, if we just have a couple of testimonies, I won't have to preach, and we can all get out of here pretty quickly." Doc knew that no one else in that building could speak English. Even the translator was going to translate from Spanish to Aguaruna. Finally one of us went up front and gave his testimony, and Doc translated it to Spanish and the translator to Aguaruna. Then a second team member went up and gave another testimony. Then our Peruvian friend played a song on his guitar. Doc said in English, "This is good, just a few more." We obliged as several more of us went up and told of what Jesus had done in our lives to that candlelit crowd.

Finally, Canisio got up and talked to them briefly and gave an invitation to accept Jesus. I was blown away as I watched ten barefoot Aguaruna walk down that center aisle up to the front and become Christians that night. Certainly it was not by any enthusiastic eloquence on our part or by any inspiring attitude we were all feeling. We were gassed, and honestly we were checked out before we set foot in there. But God had a different plan for ten individuals that night and somehow used the truth of His transforming power through our reluctant shells to change their eternities. I will never forget the lesson the Lord taught me that night.

> "Not by might nor by power, but by My Spirit," says the Lord of Hosts.
> —Zechariah 4:6B

CHAPTER 6

How Did That Get in My Bag?

The time had come. We were finally ready to go. Dave had secured our paperwork at the Sudanese embassy in Washington, DC, after much effort and prayer. It was truly a miracle just to get permission for the proper paperwork. "In all our years, we have never been able to get JESUS Film equipment into Sudan," we heard from Campus Crusade. With the Lord's direction, Dave and I were going to try and be the first.

We had heard the stories coming out of Khartoum. We knew that Condoleezza Rice's bodyguards had been roughed up a bit by airport security on a recent visit there. But we also knew from experience that our bodyguards came from a higher authority. We had taken JESUS Film equipment into other countries before, but we had a feeling that Sudan was to be a totally different animal.

The equipment we were taking with us on this occasion used a DVD format. The DVDs of the JESUS Film were unmarked for security reasons, and we would keep them in our personal backpacks. Dave and I discussed throwing in a couple of extra random DVDs into the equipment bags for some reason. We settled on *Snow White and the Seven Dwarfs* and *The Apple Dumpling Gang*[1] and threw them in on top of some of the equipment in the bags, and off we went.

We flew out of Dulles and over through Europe with one final stop in Cairo, Egypt, before hitting the final leg to Khartoum. When we stopped in Cairo, just about the whole plane emptied out, except for just a few people. It was then I realized that hardly anyone goes to Khartoum. Dave and I took the time to pray on that final leg for God's will to be done. We didn't know what to expect because we had never been there before, but we knew God had a purpose and plan to start reaching the people of this great country who had suffered so long with the Gospel. If He didn't have a plan, we never would have gotten this far.

We landed in the early morning hours. There were only a handful of us on the flight, so it didn't take long to get off the plane with our backpacks and make our way inside the terminal. As we approached the immigration desk and I handed my passport to the man behind the glass, I found it somewhat ironic as I heard a small transistor radio playing the old song from the '80s "We Are the World" from a shelf behind the glass.

He stamped us in, and we walked right into the baggage claim area. As we waited for our bags to come out, I scanned the large room. There were baggage X-ray machines and tables to search luggage and another room just off that area with a glass window dividing it from the area where we were. You could see into that room through the glass, and it was full of luggage, boxes, and electronics. I realized that everything in that room had been confiscated by airport

---

[1] *Snow White and the Seven Dwarfs* and *The Apple Dumpling Gang*, copyright Walt Disney Co.

security who were running this show. That's when we noticed that all the airport security were actually all Sudanese military.

Sudan was still in the midst of a civil war at this time. It was the Tribal South who were trying to claim independence pitted against the Muslim North, who were trying to hang onto the oil-rich South for a variety of reasons. Khartoum was in the north, which empowered these airport soldiers to confiscate anything they decided in the name of "national security." It wasn't looking too good for us at this point.

By the time our bags came out on the carousel, the rest of the other passengers (all four or five of them) were processed and gone, leaving Dave and me with about fifteen to twenty Sudanese soldiers and several bags of JESUS Film equipment. In other airports around the world, there was sometimes an option or way to circumvent going through an X-ray machine, and we would always look for that option. The Khartoum airport did not offer that option.

There were military personnel stationed at every point, and they escorted us through the whole process. Reluctantly we put our bags full of electronics on the belt and watched them go through the X-ray machine. Sure enough, the soldier who was watching the screen told us to put all the bags on the search tables to be inspected by hand. Dave and I stood there with our backpacks still hanging on our shoulders as they opened the first bag on the table. They weren't sure what they were looking at inside that bag, so they called over their captain.

The captain was a shorter man who didn't seem too thrilled to be assigned to airport detail, especially at around 2:00 a.m., and his mood was about to get worse. He came over and looked into the open bag and immediately began asking questions in his broken English. "What is this?"

We would answer, "It is film equipment for the people of Sudan."

He wasn't going for it. "Open another bag!" he barked at his soldiers. So they did. The second bag had sound equipment in it. Again he barked, "What is this?" By this time, the rest of the soldiers had come over to watch the show since we were the only ones there.

Again we answered, "It is equipment for the people of Sudan." You could feel the steam coming out of this captain as our answers weren't satisfying him.

With the help of the Lord, Dave and I remained calm, with our backpacks still hanging on our shoulders. One of the soldiers stepped up to try to calm the captain down a bit and actually vouched for us, saying, "These men are not bad men, they're alright." I've never seen this guy before in my life, and I'm pretty sure Dave hadn't either, but he was going to bat for us for some reason. The only thing I can figure is he either knew his captain's temperament and was trying to save him from an international incident on cable news, or the Lord nudged him into the fray to take the pressure off of us. I choose the second option.

The captain ordered another bag to be opened. Again more equipment. He was ready to explode. He reminded me of the Sudanese version of a Major Hochstetter from *Hogan's Heroes*.[2] Our newfound friend continued to tell him we were OK as the captain ordered another bag opened.

With all fifteen to twenty soldiers eagerly watching that next bag open, as the zipper opened up and the top cover was peeled back, lo and behold there was a DVD of *Snow White and the Seven Dwarfs* sitting right on top of the equipment. All of the soldiers began to laugh except for one. Our newfound friend told the captain in between chuckles, "You see, I told you these guys were alright."

The captain, embarrassed in front of his subordinates, looked at Dave and me and said through his teeth, "You get these bags, and you get out of here!"

We looked down and simply replied, "Yes, sir." We couldn't zip up those bags fast enough and get out of there. The whole time our backpacks containing the JESUS Film DVDs hung off our shoulders and were never X-rayed or searched.

Our contacts met us outside the terminal, and we rejoiced together at the wonder of God and His ways as soon as the airport was in our rearview mirror. It was the Lord Who orchestrated all of

---

[2] *Hogan's Heroes*, copyright of Paramount.

it, right down to the details of throwing in a couple of random DVDs ahead of time. Who would have ever imagined that the Creator of the universe would use Snow White to get His eternal Word into a country so spiritually dark?

> But God has chosen the foolish things of the world to put to shame the wise, and God has chosen the weak things of the world to put to shame the things which are mighty.
> —1 Corinthians 1:27

CHAPTER 7

EARTHQUAKE

Natural disasters have always existed since the fall of man. It's one of those things that we struggle to understand when they happen. But through them, we can see the worst of mankind and the best of mankind be expressed. One through selfishness and the other through sacrifice for others. When a 7.7 earthquake hit El Salvador, killing hundreds and leaving thousands homeless, we decided to help out.

Six of us flew down to San Salvador and then traveled outside the city to the town of Usulután, where much of the damage had taken place. We crossed a couple of rivers along the way. We met our contact who was in charge of the projects we were going to work on. Our task was to rebuild homes for families and anyone who had basically lost everything.

As we traveled around the area where our motel was located, you could see the devastation. It was road after road of piles of rubble and cleaned-off slabs with one door jamb being the only thing left standing. We pulled into our humble little motel that was surrounded by a high fence crowned with rows of razor wire. The parking lot was patrolled by several guards with Uzis hanging off their shoulders. I was beginning to wonder what we had gotten ourselves into. The only other people staying at the motel were foreign doctors and military who had been in that area as part of the first responder wave.

We were briefed on our assignment as we settled in. The church had set up a factory in neighboring Guatemala, where they were mass-producing a type of prefab house. They came in four panels that were constructed in chain-link fence material. Each one had a front wall with a door opening and window, a back wall with a window, and two side walls that had peaked gables built into them forming a simple pitch for the roofs. Then simple trusses made from rebar would fill in the roof structure and tin roofing would finish it out.

They were simple one-room homes that were about 16' by 24' with 8' tall walls. They resembled giant dog runs, but they were a quick shelter. Many of the rough structures had already been put up. Our job was to put a plywood form on the inside and another on the outside of the walls, sandwiching the chain-link fencing in-between, and then mix and pour concrete into the form to create smooth concrete walls that made the chain link sections disappear. This made an extremely strong structure when finished. The deal was made with many of the locals that they had to help build at least five of these units, and then one would be built for them.

As we set out of our compound on the first day, one of our guys was told to take off the colored bandana he was wearing. Apparently, it was the wrong color for the criminal gang that was in control of that part of the country and too dangerous to be seen wearing. I guess the last river we crossed put us in their territory. This bit of information kept us alert to our surroundings and our attire. We climbed into the back of the pickup and headed out.

When we arrived at the first site, we had a couple of locals working with us. One was a boy who was about twelve or thirteen. We soon got into a rhythm. We would put the forms on the bottom four feet all the way around the house and then mix and pour it solid. Then we would go to another house and take forms off that had been poured the day before and reset them to do the top four feet. We had several houses going at a time. With each house we worked on, this young boy worked with us.

The devastation we saw tucked back in these communities is indescribable. You would look over into the back corner of a property at a pile of junk with a tarp over it, and suddenly someone would emerge from under the tarp. That was what the people were living in. They had nothing. Yet as we worked, these older widows would come over to us with little baggies of soda in them and offer them to us to drink in gratitude for us being there. It was the best they had and basically all they had. It reminded me of the widow who gave her two mites for her offering. Of course, it was an honor to drink it.

One morning, we arrived in one community, and the people knew we were coming and somehow had giant ice cream cones waiting for us. It was eight o'clock in the morning, and these ladies were running over to us with ice cream already starting to melt and running down their forearms. I looked around and couldn't figure out where they got ice cream like this and wondered how safe it was going to be to eat it. But the joy in the face that presented it to me couldn't be turned down. I said a little prayer for safety over it, looked at the rest of the guys sucking theirs down, and figured if one of us gets sick, we're all going down. I dove in. I must admit it was pretty good even at 8:00 a.m. None of us felt any after effects—praise the Lord!

We had a chance to worship with the local church over the weekend. The church was packed. They called us up front and lined us up to face the congregation. Then many of the people came up front and laid their hands on us to pray for us. These were the people who had lost everything, and yet they were the ones praying over us. We had some fun with them after the service. One of the guys had brought a Polaroid camera with him, and once the people saw what it was producing, it was all we could do to get out of there before sundown.

Our work days were long but fruitful. I don't know for sure how many of those houses we worked on, but we knew several of them were for these aged widows. I think special allowances were made for them since they weren't able to physically help in the construction.

The last house we worked on was for a family that had about six daughters and one son. The son turned out to be the young man who had been working with us the previous week. He had finally earned his house for his family and had a larger-than-normal smile on his face as we worked on this one.

Before we left El Salvador, we visited the site just outside of San Salvador where a mudslide had instantly killed hundreds of people during the earthquake. We shed some tears and had a time of prayer before we left. We can never make sense of disasters like this, and we never will. This world is broken and always will be until Jesus comes back physically to adjust a few things. But we have the ability to be used by Jesus now to help Him readjust some of the broken pieces in the people around us if we're willing. Of course, those people in that area of El Salvador will never have the same life they had before the earthquake. Hopefully they witnessed some of the good that could come through the sacrifice of others like a twelve-year-old brother or a widow who offered her best. I know I did. And that's a change for the better.

> And He saw also a certain widow putting in two mites. So He said, "Truly I say to you that this poor widow has put in more than all; for all these out of their abundance have put in offerings for God, but she out of her poverty put in all the livelihood that she had."
> —Luke 21:2–4

CHAPTER 8

NIGHT OF THE HYENA

One of the places in Ethiopia that we needed to build a District Training Center was the small city of Awassa. Awassa is located in Southern Ethiopia right next to Lake Awassa. It takes a pretty good day's drive from the capital of Addis Ababa to reach this area. It was a large project that would take a couple of Work & Witness teams to get it up.

During a Sunday on one of these trips, the local pastor had asked me to speak. I was all prepared, and the team was ready to go to the service, but then on the way, we were informed that we would go to a baptism service first at Lake Awassa. And oh, by the way, "We want you to do that service as well," they told me.

"Not a problem," I replied. I just wish I had brought a towel or change of clothes or something.

After a short devotional on the shoreline, I began to wade out into the lake. I was to be assisted by an English-speaking Ethiopian brother who was from another part of Ethiopia and was not familiar with the Awassa area. As we waded deeper into the lake together, I asked him, "Have you seen how big the crocodiles are in this lake?"

His eyes widened and his back stiffened a bit as he gave me his unconfident answer of, "No."

I said, "I hear they're huge, but we have plenty of eyes on the shoreline to alert us." I don't think that eased his mind any.

It wasn't until after we had baptized twenty to thirty people that I finally told him that there were no crocodiles in Lake Awassa. It sure makes you feel alive if you think otherwise. I knew payback might be tough for that one, and it wasn't having to preach or spending the rest of the day in a wet pair of pants.

One of the teams brought my lovely wife, Angie, there to work on the center. It happened to be during the Muslim holy days of Ramadan. Our hotel room for the week was level with the loudspeakers of the minaret tower of the mosque next door to the hotel. These are speakers loud enough for the whole city to hear. During Ramadan, they would go off constantly for calls to prayer. You can imagine how pleasant that was, even with the earplugs I now took everywhere. Nothing but the best for my wife.

Due to time restraints on the job site and logistics with the team, it was best to bring supplies for team lunches. This would save a lot of time and get more work done while the sun was up. So the team would pack peanut butter and jelly and other items like that, and we would purchase local bread and just make enough sandwiches on site at lunchtime to eat and get back to work.

One day near the end of the project, our supplies were running out, and there happened to be a lot of local people on the site that day. As Angie and the ladies were discreetly whipping up some sandwiches for us with our depleted supplies, we noticed all these new people jumped in line with us unannounced. A couple of the ladies saw the potential problem arising, and Angie asked, "What should we do?"

We didn't want to turn them away, but we also didn't want to run out of food halfway through the line. So we decided to make as many as we could and see what happens. We should've run out, but we didn't. We had enough for everyone that day. It was one of those moments when God said, "I've got this." And why not? He's done it before. Some things you just don't try to figure out.

An opportunity came up to be involved in a JESUS Film showing while this work team was there. It was going to be held in a village outside of Awassa that we hadn't been to. So I left early one day to set out and find this village where the showing was to take place. It was about thirty minutes away and off the beaten path. I locked the coordinates in my mind once I found it. I took the vehicle back to the job site and finished the workday.

After the team had eaten a quick dinner and had cleaned up, we loaded up into two older Land Rover–type vehicles and got ready to set out of town in search of this village. Since I was the one who had located this village just a few hours ago, I drove the first vehicle. Dave was riding shotgun with me and had his window down. Angie was riding in the second vehicle with a few of the other women.

I put that four on the floor stick shift in gear, and we headed out of Awassa and into the dark African night. The very dark African night. Did I mention it was dark? There were no lights once you got away from Awassa, and whatever coordinates that were so confidently locked into my head just a few short hours before were beginning to unravel. Nothing looked familiar to me as we traveled down the road.

The only thing I was sure about now was that we had to turn off the road to the right at some point, and the village would be out in the bush aways. I tried to guess how long we had been traveling and sync it with the earlier trip I made. We were soon out in the bush with both vehicles. That's when I wondered if I should say anything or just keep going. How hard could it be to find a village? We just kept going.

The terrain was getting rougher, and you couldn't see lights anywhere. That's when I may have mentioned, "It's gotta be around here somewhere." I'm sure the second vehicle was trying to figure out how far this village could be at this point. That's when I saw all these lights. It looked like a bunch of headlights facing us in front. But there was something very strange about these lights. That's when I realized they weren't headlights at all but dozens of eyeballs attached to a large pack of hyenas!

All sorts of things run through your mind in situations like this. One was headlines on the nightly news across America of a group of volunteers who got lost in Ethiopia, due to the stupidity of their driver, and were eaten by a pack of savage hyenas. Another thought was, *Have you seen how big the crocodiles are in this lake?* I told you the payback would be tough.

I wasn't the only one uneasy at this point. We went through a jarring rut in the ground, and some object flipped up and hit Dave's door. He practically jumped into my lap from the passenger seat, knocking the vehicle out of gear. He only said, "I thought a hyena got me," as he settled back into his seat and was rolling up his window.

We drove on a bit farther as I was wondering who was going to explain to our kids the demise of their parents, when we saw a distant glow. I turned toward it and drove on. It happened to be the village we were looking for. This glow was the light emanating through the vertical stick walls of the local church. They were all set up and wondering where we had been. A comment might have been made about how bad the traffic was. Either way, I was relieved as were the others, and we had a good JESUS Film showing to that local community.

What a difference between the warm glow of the lights coming from the church and the piercing light coming from those eyeballs.

Those eyes were not a source of light but only a reflection from our headlights. There is a big difference. We live in a world with so much false light. It's quite a comfort knowing the One Who is the source of true Light. For the record, we made it back to Awassa later that night without any problems.

> Then Jesus spoke to them again saying, "I Am the Light of the world. He who follows Me shall not walk in darkness, but have the Light of life."
>
> —John 8:12

CHAPTER 9

WELCOME BACK, BOYS

Well it worked out so well the first time, Dave and I thought, *Why not try it again?* There was still a great need for more JESUS Film equipment within Sudan. We had heard that the film teams were really using the first two sets we took in just a few months earlier. We were willing to go again, but what did God have in mind? The answer would be in securing a second visa to enter the country. It was a miracle to get a visa for two Americans for one trip but totally unheard of to secure a second visa within a few months' time.

God opened the door, as only He could have, and Dave and I were soon making plans to take another run at the customs officials in Khartoum. We had a Work & Witness project set up in neighboring Ethiopia that a team of guys was ready to do. Our plan was to leave a few days before the team, fly to Sudan, and drop off two more sets of JESUS Film equipment, then fly to Addis Ababa and meet up with the work team when they arrived from the States.

Dave and I packed our bags and headed out. We landed in another part of the world and prepared for the last leg of our flight to Khartoum. Once again, the plane emptied out, except for a select few. Having just experienced this trip a few months before, we kind of knew what to expect, and yet we didn't. What we did know was that God was there the last time, and we prayed He would show up again this time. We also prayed that He would blind the eyes of all the guards who were going to be working the shift when we would arrive.

We landed and disembarked to head to the terminal, praying the whole way. As I approached the immigration official, there was no music playing on his transistor radio like last time. As he looked over my paperwork, I glanced over my left shoulder to take a quick peek at the customs area to see if anything had changed in the last couple of months. It had not. The official stamped my passport and handed it back to me, and Dave and I were soon waiting for all our bags to be brought off the plane.

We collected them and made our way to the gauntlet of customs that was still being run by the Sudanese military. But something was different this time. There seemed to be more of a peace over the whole atmosphere in the room. I never saw "Major Hochstetter" who had grilled us on our previous visit. I didn't know if he was just off that evening or had been transferred to another post. I didn't ask.

We were still guided to the X-ray machines and were told to put all of our bags, through which we did. But this time, we weren't asked any questions or made to open up the bags on the search tables. We had brought *Snow White* and *The Apple Dumpling Gang* again, but they never saw the light of day. We grabbed our bags and loaded them on our carts and went out the doors of the airport and into the Sahara heat. It was as if they never saw a thing. Two more sets of JESUS Film equipment that would share the Gospel with thousands were now safely in Sudan.

Our Sudanese contacts were there to pick us up as well as our buddy Friday. Friday was a Kenyan who was called as a missionary to other parts of Africa. He and his wife, Mary, actually sold their family cow to raise enough money to be able to go to the mission field. We had worked with Friday a number of times in Ethiopia and had become quite close. He was now setting up shop in Sudan to help with the fast-paced church growth.

We climbed into Friday's vehicle with all our equipment and praised the Lord for His goodness and what He had done again in getting us through customs. We forgot to ask the Lord to reopen the eyes of those officials…I hope they're OK. So we had the chance to spend the next couple of days in Khartoum before heading over to Ethiopia to meet up with the soon-arriving work team.

This time, we had wheels since Friday was there. With money that had been raised, he was able to purchase a used Toyota Land Cruiser that had every window tinted out, even the windshield. There was only a strip of about six to eight inches at eye level out the windshield that was not blacked out. No one could see into the vehicle.

I noticed that as we drove around the streets of the city that every time we passed military personnel, and there were quite a bit, they would snap to attention and salute our vehicle as we would drive by. Apparently only high-ranking officials own vehicles like this in Sudan, and Friday must have purchased this one from someone important. It was kinda nice to have all these guys salute us after what they put us through the first time we visited. They couldn't see me, but I would always try to salute back to them. I figured it was just courteous.

We had the chance to do and see a few things in Khartoum during our short stay there. We saw where the Blue Nile and the White Nile come together to form the Nile River as it heads north to Egypt. We also had a chance to attend a *whirling dervish* that took place in a Muslim cemetery. I don't recommend that one, spiritually speaking.

One place we went during the day was the open market downtown. This is where the locals shop. I had expected to see all the spices and local wares that were laid out before us. What I didn't expect to see was a table full of beautiful red apples. As I was drawn closer, I thought, *Where in the world could they have gotten apples out here in the middle of this sand pit?* I picked one up out of its organized rack and noticed it had a little sticker on it that said "Washington State." With the embargoes in place at that time, these apples shouldn't have been here, but they were. That's when it hit me that embargoes don't change countries. There will always be black markets. If you truly want to change a country, you have to change it one heart at a time. That change only comes with the transforming power of Jesus Christ.

When we left the market, Dave and I had the chance to meet with different groups at different locations on the outskirts of Khartoum. These groups were refugees from Southern Sudan, and the meeting places were the unfinished shells of houses or buildings that most of them were living in as squatters for the time being. They heard we were coming and would invite all their neighbors to come over and listen to what the foreigners had to say.

Dave and I would take turns sharing with them. It reminded me of something out of the Book of Acts. I remember finishing up at one of these gatherings when one of the men there stood up and asked me through the interpreter, "Why has God forgotten us?" All forty heads in the room turned and looked right at me for an answer. In a split second, many thoughts raced through my mind including, "Why wasn't it Dave's turn to share with this group?"

I also thought that I could never relate or even come close to understanding what these people have seen or experienced in the last twenty years of civil war in their country. How could this white boy from Virginia answer this deep and sincere question from a man who obviously wanted God to answer him for quite a while?

All this in a split second, and then in the rest of that second, I felt the Lord drop the answer in my head and had it coming out of my mouth as I found myself saying, "God's people in the Old Testament had the very same question. For four hundred years, they struggled with being enslaved and then spent another forty years wandering around a desert. Many of them wondered why God had forgotten them, but He didn't. He had a land waiting for them—a promised land flowing with milk and honey, and He was with them for every step. For what you have gone through these last twenty years, He must have something truly special waiting for all of you." He smiled and shook his head as did the other forty heads in the room. So did I. It was a long but fruitful day.

Before we flew out to Ethiopia, we were asked to speak at different churches. Dave and Friday and I would split up and go in different directions with our own interpreters, and each of us would speak at a different church. When I arrived at my assigned church, the structure there had most of three of its walls but no fourth wall and no roof. There were about one hundred people in attendance who are the true church anyway. All of the people were refugees from South Sudan. It didn't matter that there was no sound system or only a few benches. We had our hands to clap and our voices to sing, and we had a great time worshipping the Lord together.

Imagine my surprise to find out that this church and the others, where Dave and Friday were speaking, were all started from JESUS Film showings on the first two sets of equipment that the Lord allowed us to get into Sudan just a few short months before this visit. I was absolutely humbled to be able to speak to a church of new believers knowing I had been a small part of their new life in Christ. Perhaps the Lord is beginning to change another country one heart at a time. I guess God has something very special waiting for all of us sometimes.

> I will build My church, and the gates of hades shall not prevail against it.
> —Matthew 16:18B

CHAPTER 10

You Can't Get There from Here

An opportunity arose to help with a new program that was aimed to train pastors and church leaders in India on how to use the JESUS Film in a different way. It was a partnership between Campus Crusade (now known as Cru) and Harvest Partners (a Nazarene-affiliated JESUS Film Ministry). The focus of the strategy was how to reach the upper caste Hindus in the local communities with the Gospel.

The problem was that only the lower caste Hindus in India would come out publicly together to watch the film. With the caste system still entrenched in India, the upper caste will have nothing to do with the lower caste and in turn would not come out for the public showings. So the issue was how to reach them as well. It was known that the upper caste households were better off financially, and most of those households owned a VCR (it was a while ago). The focus shifted from large public showings of the film to smaller groups in houses and smaller venues through tape showings of the JESUS Film.

My assignment would be to travel from one organized training assembly to another in various Indian cities. We would then train hundreds of pastors and Christian leaders at a time from all different denominations with these new techniques. This was back when we still used travel agents, so I called mine up and told her I needed to get to Bangalore, India. I would be traveling alone and meeting up with a small group of other trainers when I arrived. I was booked and packed as light as I could and soon headed off to the airport.

My first leg took me through Amsterdam and then on to Mumbai (Bombay), India. I arrived in Mumbai at about 2:00 a.m. I was supposed to switch airlines and catch a domestic flight from Mumbai to the southern city of Bangalore, but I had a little bit of time. It was a good thing. I couldn't find this other domestic airline anywhere in this airport. I went back and forth with no luck at all. Finally I asked an agent who worked there where I could find the desk for this airline. She told me, "That airline isn't in this airport. It's at the domestic airport."

That prompted my next question, "Where's the domestic airport?"

Her reply was, "On the other side of Mumbai" Not an encouraging answer at 2:00 a.m. and no airport shuttle of any kind.

I had heard the stories of how Westerners had disappeared in situations like this in a city of over sixteen million. They unwittingly would put their trust in the wrong people to drive them around and then vanish. After a bit of prayer, I stepped out of the airport to a sea of eager taxi drivers. I looked them over and picked out one that I thought I could take if he tried anything nefarious. He must have been the smallest and skinniest taxi driver in the whole city. But he did get me to the domestic airport with a few minutes to spare. I thanked him and the Lord for watching over me. I was in Bangalore a few hours later.

I was picked up by our contacts with Campus Crusade and taken to their headquarters. There were eight of us in this program. After some brief training sessions, we were sent out two by two to different regions of India. I was teamed up with a college-aged guy named Josh. Our region was the major cities on the East Coast of India. The assemblies were all planned in advance. All we had to do was show up and train the hundreds who would be there.

Josh and I headed east by train to Chennai (Madras) and then went to the airport to fly north. Before we left, I was handed a good-sized box packed with JESUS Film VHS tapes in a particular East Indian language. They told me that the tapes were to pass out at the first assembly when we got there because they thought they might not have enough on-site for the expected crowd. Getting it on the train was no problem. Now I had to get it on a plane without raising suspicions about what was in the box. Hindu officials don't take too kindly to Christian evangelism.

As we went through the screening process, sure enough, that box got flagged. They asked me to follow them into a side room. I left Josh out in the lobby and followed the uniformed gentlemen with the box. We entered the private side room that was equipped with an X-ray machine. As they loaded the box on the belt to go through the machine, they turned to me and asked me what was in it. I said, "VHS tapes."

It went through the machine. They grabbed it as it came out, flipped it over, loaded it back on the belt, and sent it on its way again through the X-ray machine. After that, they grabbed it again, flipped it on its side this time, and sent it again. And as they proceeded to do it again for a fourth time, they asked me again, "What's in the box?" I said, "VHS tapes"—nothing more, nothing less. They said, "OK, you can take it and go." I couldn't believe they never opened it. I was almost afraid to pick up the box at this point after being x-rayed so much, thinking it might be a bit radioactive.

I checked the box of JESUS Film tapes in with our airline, and we flew about halfway up the east coast of India to a city called Visakhapatnam (I know, I didn't know how to say it either). Our training sessions went well. Josh and I shared the duties, and I did most of the speaking. We didn't stay in one place for too long, and on some days, we did multiple events. In one of the cities we went to, our local Campus Crusade drivers dropped us off ten feet from a side entrance door. We were instructed to go in and start right away. Then as soon as we were finished with the training, we were to immediately go out that door. They said that there would be a running vehicle waiting for us.

We did as instructed, and when we entered that side door, there were several hundred trainees already seated and ready. It wasn't until we were whisked away in a huff that we found out that particular city was the headquarters for the most radical and violent Hindu movement in India. They had eyes everywhere. I guess Josh and I were on a need-to-know basis.

Our schedule kept us pretty busy, but we were able to stop from time to time in between these well-attended speaking engagements. One time, our driver stopped so we could get a picture of ourselves in front of some sacred Hindu site. We were chased away by a volley of stones from those thinking we were desecrating the site. I still have that picture.

On the flip side of that story, we had a long stretch of travel between cities and were going through an extremely remote area when our Campus Crusade hosts told us that there was a JESUS Film team in this area and asked if we wanted to detour for a few minutes to meet them. These teams sacrifice so much to do this ministry, so of course, we wanted to meet them.

We soon pulled off that so-called main road and went back down some pathways through some very small villages. After a few turns, we stopped when the vehicle couldn't go any further. We got out and started walking. As we walked unannounced through this village in the middle of nowhere, I saw a woman holding a bag of grain of some type, and she definitely saw us.

She stood there frozen. Her mouth was wide open, and her eyes weren't blinking. She kept repeating something in her local dialect, but never took her eyes off of us as we walked on. I thought that was strange because she looked petrified. Then a boy of about nine or ten came running out in front of us, proclaiming in broken English, "She think you gods, she think you gods!"

Then I knew things were getting strange. I also knew that I couldn't approach her or say anything that wouldn't freak her out. Josh and I agreed we shouldn't stay long. I assured the young boy that we were not gods, but I wasn't confident that he would pass that detail on to the rest of the village.

We found the JESUS Film team and had a brief but very encouraging visit with this group of guys. We had prayer with them and made our way briskly back out of that village and got back on the road. That was more than creepy, but at least no rocks were thrown at us this time.

We arrived early at our next venue. It was to be held on a large covered parapet or flat roof. All the chairs were set up, and the local crew was finishing up the sound checks before the trainees would start arriving. As we waited, I walked over to the edges of the parapet and was able to look down on the street and people walking by. As I made my way around the edge to the back side of the building, I was able to look down into the adjoining property.

It was the back side of the property of a small manufacturing outfit that made statues of Hindu gods. Up front, they would sell them. But out here in the back, where no patron could see, were all the broken pieces and statues that came out misshapen or defective. They were piled up in random scrap heaps and discarded. I thought of the irony of the whole scene. Here I am looking down at a junkyard of the broken gods of this land, and I'm about ready to share with a couple hundred eager trainees the message of the One true God Who is alive and active and doesn't sit on a shelf. It's no wonder that God had been opening so many doors. He yearns to reach these people. I knew I was in the right place.

> Look to Me, and be saved, all you ends of
> the earth! For I AM God, and there is no other.
> —Isaiah 45:22

CHAPTER 11

HUAMBISA

In all the times and trips we had been with Doc Garman in the jungles of Peru, and there had been a few, we mostly worked and stayed with the tribal people called the Aguaruna. Doc and his wife, Addie, had been ministering to them for over forty years in the headwaters of the Amazon River. It made sense that almost all of our projects would be in one of these Aguaruna villages.

But the project Doc had for us this time was not with the Aguaruna. It was a project with a different tribe called the Huambisa. It was the team's first experience with this indigenous group, but first, we had to get to where they were.

The typical trip to get to the mission station where the Garmans lived was as follows: fly to Lima from the States, fly from Lima up the coast of Peru to the coastal town of Chiclayo, get the team in a rented bus and drive all day from Chiclayo, over the Andes Mountains, to a town on the edge of the Amazon Jungle, and then hire out vehicles with armed guards (due to bandit activity) for several more bone-rattling hours on a "jungle road" to the mission station on the banks of the Marañón River. That process got you to the Garman's house.

Once we made it to the mission station and rested a bit, we would then load up our gear on a couple of open motorized johnboats and start our trek down the Marañón to wherever our projects would be. If they were a good ways off, we would sometimes stay in a jungle town called Nieva. It took about six hours by boat to reach Nieva downriver and about eight hours to get back upriver from Nieva to the mission station. The Huambisa weren't that close.

Once we loaded up the boats at the mission station for this particular trip, we would end up spending over thirty hours on them to reach the first village. At least they were in the same jungle. As we traveled down the Marañón River, we would occasionally pass another boat or two loaded down with basic supplies heading somewhere to unload their cargo. We'd sometimes pass powered dugout canoes with local Indians occupying them on their way to hunt or fish somewhere in the jungle.

One of the strangest things I ever saw in the rivers was an object swimming across a rather wide portion of the river. As we got closer to it, we realized that it was a pig, and he was making great progress. I thought, *What in the world?* I've heard rumors that they might be able to fly, but now I know that they can definitely swim. Who knows what might have chased him into the water…he may not have had a choice.

Our journey downriver eventually took us to the mouth of another main Amazon tributary called the Morona River. We turned left and our downriver experience turned into an upriver one as we began our way up this mighty river. The farther we traveled, the less people we would see. Not that we saw a bunch of people out there to begin with. We would go hours without seeing a single soul. We had left the territory of the Aguaruna and had entered the realm of the Huambisa.

As we continued, we would occasionally have to pull off and stop at a few random checkpoints that the Peruvian military had set up. They would check our passports and ask a few questions but would basically wave us through. For fun one time, we shuffled up our passports and passed them out randomly to the team so everyone had someone else's passport just to see if the guards at the checkpoint would notice. I'm still writing so you can conclude that they didn't pick up on this rouse.

Our trip wore on as the sun was going down. It's too dangerous to travel on the rivers at night. You may hit debris like floating logs or an occasional swimming pig and damage your boat or worse. So we went as far as we could and pulled off to the side of the river and anchored down for the night. We were next to a beach area, but it was also too dangerous to sleep on the sand, because of a certain sand flea that lived in that area that liked to invade your body. I'll leave it at that.

Everyone on the boat tried to find a way to get comfortable for the next few hours until the sun came up. Needless to say, it was not a good night's sleep. We were even visited by a curious pink river dolphin during the night that would just swim up and bump the boats because he could. As the sun came up, we all became upright and continued our journey up the Morona River. I was beginning to think, *How in the world did Doc find out about the needs way up here?* We were inching closer and closer to Ecuador.

Finally we made it to the first Huambisa village. Nothing stood out that told me it was much different than your typical Aguaruna village. I guess if they had them, they could've shuffled their passports and handed them to me, and I would've waved them on through. We were there to build them a church like we had done so many times before in other villages. Once we finished there, we were to go to two more Huambisa villages and build two more churches. This we accomplished with the Lord's strength and safety. We discovered that these three Huambisa congregations were fairly new and growing. Then Doc told us the story behind the whole venture.

The Amazon jungle is home to many different indigenous Indian tribes. Throughout history, they haven't always treated each other too well. If one tribe felt slighted or perceived they were slighted in some way by another tribe, they would retaliate. This retaliation usually took the intensity up a notch. You can see how this could quickly escalate and also produce a spirit of paranoia as you tried to live your normal life. Sometimes these sorts of skirmishes would even happen from one village to the next within the same tribe. Before too long, you would end up with violent raids and revenge killings. It can be a vicious cycle.

Doc told us that not long ago it was alleged that an Aguaruna Indian had killed a Huambisa Indian in some type of dispute. Of course, the news of this set off the Huambisa tribe and also put the Aguaruna tribe on alert for some type of revenge. In the midst of these heightened emotions, there was one Aguaruna man who had become a Christian. He took it upon himself to go and talk to the Huambisa people. I'm sure this man was changed under the ministry of the Garmans.

This man felt the Lord leading him to make that long journey to the Huambisa territory. When he made this news public to those around him, they told him he was crazy. "The Huambisa will surely kill you in the first village you set foot in," they told him. Their pleas did not dissuade him. He decided to go anyway. After just spending thirty hours in a motorized boat to reach the Huambisa, I can't imagine how long it took this man to paddle his canoe on that same route. He certainly had plenty of time to think and pray about what he was doing and opportunity to turn back. But he didn't. The Lord had lit a fire in him.

He finally reached that first Huambisa village just like we had done weeks later. But he was met with a different greeting than ours. The Huambisa told him, "You shouldn't have come here. Someone will surely kill you!" He stayed and shared with them what Jesus Christ had done in his life and how He had changed his heart and how He offers the same love to them. Quite a number of them believed his message and accepted Jesus into their lives. The Aguaruna man stayed with them for a while, discipling them with the basics until he felt the Lord moving him on to the second Huambisa village.

Now the Huambisa from the first village were urging him not to go. They warned him, "You can't go to that village. It would be crazy. They will surely kill you when they see you!" He went anyway. When he arrived, he was greeted in much the same way the first village greeted him. "You shouldn't have come here. Someone will surely kill you!" Again, he shared the Good News of Jesus Christ with similar results. After more discipling, he then went on to the third village with the same warnings echoing in his mind. But the Lord produced the same stunning results in the third village as well.

These were the three churches we were constructing while we were there. One man defying warnings and common sense from friends and foes but listening to the prompting of the Lord to share an experience of forgiveness and love. He made an eternal impact on more people than he could ever imagine. I'm sure his long canoe ride back home was quite joyful.

> But none of these things move me; nor do I count my life dear to myself, so that I may finish my race with joy and the ministry which
> I received from the Lord Jesus, to testify to the Gospel of the grace of God.
> —Acts 20:24

CHAPTER 12

HELLO, PATAGONIA

We had recently finished up another successful trip to the Peruvian Amazon jungle with Doc. Now we had a project to work on in Argentina. We had been to Argentina before and done projects just outside of Buenos Aires and out west near Bariloche. This new project was a bit different. There was a small church in the southern coastal city of Puerto Madryn that had a burden for the street kids and underprivileged children of that city. They had been so successful in housing and feeding these children that they were now in need of a more suitable structure for education.

We had an experienced group ready to answer the call and make the long trek to the southern part of South America to build it. We all flew to Miami to wait for the big nine-hour leg to Buenos

Aires. When we were in Miami, I got word that Dave wasn't feeling too good. I knew before we left Virginia that he had been struggling recently, but now that we were on the way, he had taken a turn for the worse.

During our layover, Dave had checked himself into a room at the hotel at the Miami Airport to take a shower and try to get some private rest and shake it off a little bit before the longest part of the journey. Somehow he dragged himself onto the plane, and we were off. Once we got to the International Airport in Buenos Aires, we had to travel to the other side of that huge city to the Domestic Airport to continue our journey farther south to the Patagonia region of the country. Unlike my experience in India, at least I knew that airport switch was coming this time.

Once we arrived in Puerto Madryn and settled in, we went over to check on the project. It was going to be a big one. The building was to have a large gymnasium-type room with a very high ceiling in the center. That room would be surrounded by classrooms all around the edge of the structure. Our goal was to get as many terra-cotta blocks laid on the walls as possible during our stay.

Our team was excited the first day and really got off to a great start. Dave came out despite still being ill and lasted for a while before he had to call it a day and go back to the hotel. By that afternoon, he told his roommate, "I feel like I'm dying," and Dave was taken to the local hospital. It was great that a hospital was close by; the issue was that it looked like something out of a 1930s Soviet State.

They diagnosed Dave right away with malaria and began treatments in the ICU for him. Apparently on our most recent trip to the Amazon with Doc, Dave was bitten by an infected mosquito, and now the malaria was in full bloom. I was the only other one on this new team that had been on that Amazon team, but so far, I was still feeling fine.

We would work during the day and then take turns going over to visit Dave in the evenings. Since he was in the ICU, they would only allow two visitors at a time, and you had to basically put on a hazmat suit to go in there. Much prayer was being offered on his behalf. A few days later, we got word from Virginia that Dave's son

Bradley had come down with the same symptoms that Dave was experiencing. Bradley had also been on that Amazon team. Sure enough, he had malaria too.

I still felt fine, but it was recommended that everyone who had been on that trip should pick up malaria medication in case we started having symptoms. This way we would have it on hand to start treating the symptoms immediately if they manifested. Apparently malaria can show up soon or later depending on who is bitten. I decided to wait until I got back to the States to get my medication. I had another trip scheduled to Ethiopia with Dave's brother Glen almost immediately after getting back from Argentina, and it would be good to have the meds on hand in case I was a so-called late bloomer.

Day by day, the project took shape. We were building relationships with the local people and the children, and Dave was making progress in his recovery. I was asked to preach one night after a type of potluck dinner put on by the local people. We met in a cozy building made up mostly of corrugated metal. I remember I was speaking about Jesus and the disciples in the boat on the Sea of Galilee when the storm blew up on them. As I got to the part about the storm, a real storm blew up where we were. The wind and the rain were so loud on that metal structure that we had to wait several minutes for it to blow over. I guess God wanted some extra emphasis on the Scriptures that night.

Dave was finally moved out of the ICU and put into a regular hospital room. Out of the eight people who were in that ICU when Dave arrived, he was the only one still alive. The news got out and around that a bunch of Americans were in Puerto Madryn to work on a school for their children. A local radio station came by the job site and wanted to interview us on the radio. Two of us were picked to go. A team member named Al was one, and I was chosen to go with him.

We cleaned up as best we could and traveled across town to the radio station.

They brought us into the station and took us right into the broadcasting room. We sat around a large round table with microphones in front of us and a large red light on the center of the table. When the light came on, the announcers made some introductions in Spanish and some small talk through an interpreter about some current NBA player who happened to be from Argentina. We were also able to tell them why we were there and how Jesus had changed our lives and put the love and desire in our hearts to travel and work for kids we didn't know. The interview didn't last long after that, and we were escorted back to the job site to get back to work. We found out later that this radio station was one of the major stations for the southern part of Argentina and that its broadcast encompassed the whole bottom portion of the continent of South America coast to coast. Who knew?

By week's end, we had completed all the blockwork low and high. We got word that on the last day, a dedication ceremony was planned. As we were finishing off some final details, the locals worked feverishly to clean up the large gymnasium room that was now encased with a number of smaller classrooms. Floors were swept, chairs were set up, a speaking platform was erected, and plenty of Argentina flags and decorations were quickly hung up. Come to find out, the governor of that part of Argentina had heard what was going on in Puerto Madryn, and he was coming to share some words with the people and to thank us for coming.

It was a large crowd and a long ceremony. I'm not much into ceremonies like that, but I'm sure they have their purpose. All I know is that because a small group of Christians decided to help some kids on another continent in the name of Jesus Christ, it caught a lot of attention. We may never know how many people heard about His love near and far.

Bradley recovered from his malaria back in Virginia. Dave ended up making a full recovery as well and could probably write his own book based solely on his hospital experience. The silver lining to Dave's painful saga was that God put him in a South American hospital, as primitive as it was, that had a lot of experience with tropical diseases like malaria. They were able to diagnose him immediately with what type he had and how to treat it. We feel if Dave had not gone on this trip and happened to stay in the States instead, the local doctors in his hometown may not have pinpointed his type of illness in time or known how to immediately treat it. Dave's diagnosis also guided the doctors in how to treat Bradley. We're not sure Dave would still be with us today if God had not pushed him to Argentina.

> You will be brought before governors and kings for My sake, as a testimony to them and to the gentiles.
> —Matthew 10:18

CHAPTER 13

THE UTTERMOST

I had known Dave's brother Glen for a while now and knew he had done so much in mission work over the years in his own right. But I had never had the opportunity to travel with him before. After just returning home from Argentina, the opportunity finally came up with a scheduled trip to Ethiopia. Glen was scheduled to travel south to some very remote tribes that are still in existence and check on some ministry opportunities there. I was to travel west to a place called Gambella to check on the possibility of constructing a church for a congregation in that area. I was to meet with leadership and plan our next step in preparations.

Glen and I landed in Addis Ababa and met our field director Howie Shute. In our first meeting that night, it was determined that

Glen's trip to the south would have to be called off due to recent extensive flood damage in that area of the country. We knew that might be a possibility before we left, but the extent of the damage was unknown at that point. So we all decided to head west to Gambella.

The three of us would fly out to Gambella and meet our Kenyan buddy Friday and check out this site for this new church structure. We would also have a chance to do some ministry in that area as well. As we made our final approach into Gambella's only runway on our smaller prop plane, I realized that this was a fairly remote place. We disembarked and walked through the one-room terminal that was made of corrugated metal. We were greeted by the smiling face of Friday who picked us up.

We drove the dirt roads into Gambella and discussed what would be our itinerary for the next several days. We weren't going to be in town very long. The plan was to go even farther west and show the JESUS Film near the border of Sudan. This would require a bit more travel. We checked out the site where the future church was to be constructed, and the plans were finalized to bring in a Work & Witness team to handle it in the near future. Then we heard that another church in that area wanted to have a baptism service while we were still in town. The only place to do this was in the river that ran through Gambella and separated one side of town from the other.

That river always had a crowd because it was the only water source for miles around. The people would bathe, do laundry, let their animals cool off, wash vehicles, and use it for drinking water too. But because it was the only river close by, it was the only place for crocodiles to live as well. The day before we arrived, someone had been eaten by a croc right in this very area.

As we went to the baptism service, I waited on volunteering to help since I wasn't in charge. Friday was going to handle this one, although he was a bit apprehensive. Glen and I assured him that we would be spotters on the shoreline to make sure nothing got close.

We also told him that the crocodile had just eaten so he's probably not looking for a meal today. Friday did great even with his head on a swivel the whole time.

We picked up our JESUS Film team leader named Stephen and began to drive west. From Gambella westward, almost all of the villages and people you come across are from Sudan. Many have settled there, but a lot had been displaced due to the civil war that had been going on in Sudan for years. Stephen was also from Sudan from a tribe called the Nuer.

We drove on for a few hours and stopped in a very small village as the sun was setting. The people there were very gracious and very poor. We decided to show the JESUS Film to them that night, but first, they wanted to feed us a meal. We agreed. We knew these people didn't have much, but they fed us bushbuck (some type of small antelope) and a side of some sort of grain meal mixture. It hit the spot.

As we were sitting and eating on the ground, I looked over to see a big bag of grain that had Nazarene Compassionate Ministries (NCM) stamped on it. A few months earlier, NCM had a drive to help with the bad famine in this part of Africa, and Angie and I had given to support their efforts. I realized that not only was it delivered, but I was eating a meal from it in this remote setting.

The JESUS Film showing went well that night as these people were stunned to hear Jesus speak to them in their native tongue. Some people climbed into trees to get a better view of the whole spectacle. Many came to know the Lord that night.

After changing one of our tires, we climbed into our vehicle the next morning and continued west on this so-called road. We had many hours to go, which gave us time to converse a bit. Somehow the conversation got onto the subject of food. (I guess we were all getting a little hungry.) Stephen started telling us about the cuisine of the Nuer tribe. One dish that peaked our attention was called- cope. Stephen said the ancients would prepare this dish. It was a mixture of dried fish, some sort of meal base, and wait for it...cow urine.

I thought, *Wow! It's a good thing they made this in ancient times!* How in the world did they collect cow urine? Did a guy run around with a bucket just waiting? We soon moved on to other subjects. A few hours later as my stomach growled, I started thinking about this cope again. I was looking at the back of Stephen's head as he sat in front of me in the vehicle. I knew we were headed to a Nuer area, and I also knew English wasn't Stephen's first language. I started wondering what his definition of "the ancients" actually meant. So I said, "Hey, Stephen, are there any ancients still alive today?" He said, "Of course." His definition of ancients was older people. I didn't have any more questions for a while.

We drove on for hours until we came to the end of what was left of the dirt road. We were met there by another Sudanese man named John. He climbed in, and we continued west through the bush. John was now our guide. He was also a pastor of several churches out here in the bush that he would circuit ride to minister to. We also noticed that John didn't look too well. We drove on and on through the bush.

We finally came to a very small village where we planned to spend the night. As we pulled out our one-man tents to set up in a clearing, a pickup truck appeared out of nowhere. It was full of men. Each one had an AK-47 hanging off their shoulders. I thought, *This could be interesting.*

They wanted to know who we were and what we were doing there. We simply told them we were there to show a film to the local people. Come to find out, these guys were Sudanese rebels who patrolled this area (even though we were technically still in Ethiopia, I think). They said we should have reported to them, but "Go ahead with your plans." We thanked them and assured them that the next time we were in the area, we'll check with them first.

We continued to set up, and John tried to get in the shade to rest. It was extremely hot in that area. Hot enough to melt my Speed Stick into liquid in its container. I don't know the melting point of Speed Stick, and I don't want to know. Even though we were sweating a lot, John's sweat was different. You could tell he wasn't right. His eyes were also yellow. That's a sure sign that he had malaria in the past and was currently dealing with it again.

That's when I realized I still had that malaria medication with me that I had picked up when I got home from Argentina. I dug it out and went to talk with John. I told him how to take it and gave it to him. Perhaps God put me in this uttermost part of the world just so He could save Pastor John's life.

After we had set up that afternoon, a goat was brought out and paraded in front of us as if they wanted to sell it to us. They then staked it up near our tents for a while before it disappeared. If you haven't guessed yet, it was to be part of dinner. They had chopped its head off and thrown the head onto the thin thatch roof of a nearby hut. They took the rest of the goat and chopped it up and boiled it in a large pot.

They called us to that same hut for dinner not long after. In that culture, the men eat first sitting in a circle on the ground around a communal pot in the hut. Each man was given his own utensil, and you would fish out what you wanted, a bite at a time. The first pot came in, and it was a white mealy dish with chunks in it. Wouldn't you know this village still had some ancients around. It was cope. I ate what I could and watched Glen and Friday dig holes in the section of the pot in front of them with their local spoons. They looked like they ate it, but I'm pretty sure it never touched their lips.

Then the next pot was brought in. It was the goat all chopped up and in the pot. As we were digging through that pot, I happened to look up, and the goat's head was still on that thin thatch roof face down, eyes open, watching us eat him. I elbowed Glen to check it out.

We slept as well as we could that night in our separate tents. I was the first one up the next morning, and as I crawled out of my tent to greet the new day, I was greeted by a man standing over me with an AK-47. Not quite sure if he was friend or foe. After a quick prayer, I said the first thing that came to my mind. "Do you know where the local Denny's is?" He had no idea what I said. He just smiled. I took that as a good sign. I found out later that he had been left by the Sudanese rebels to guard us through the night. I wish they had told me about that.

That night, we helped Stephen set up to show the JESUS Film here in the middle of nowhere. Pastor John was already getting more energy back and helping too. As the sun went down, we started the film with a few hundred in attendance as people kept coming. The locals laughed at first watching these white men on the screen speaking fluently in their language. It wasn't long before the laughter turned into serious attention as the life of Jesus unfolded before them.

Meanwhile, people kept coming. I didn't know where they were coming from. This village didn't have this many people. The crowd swelled to over a thousand. After the crucifixion and resurrection scenes, an invitation to accept Jesus was given, and hundreds came forward. All these people who kept coming by foot throughout the movie were from other villages. Some of them miles away. In less than twenty-four hours, they got word of this event and made the sacrifice and dangerous journey to see Jesus.

Besides the hundreds of people saved that night, three churches were planted in three different villages. Pastor John added these new churches to the several other churches he was already ministering to. All that from one JESUS Film showing. Even in the uttermost regions of the world, God is there and showing up for those who are willing to look for Him.

> Where can I go from Your Spirit? Or where can I flee from Your Presence? If I ascend into heaven, You are there; If I make my bed in hell, behold, You are there. If I take the wings of the morning, and dwell in the uttermost parts of the sea, even there Your hand shall lead me, and Your right hand shall hold me.
> —Psalm 139:7–10

CHAPTER 14

THE TORCH

Gambella, Ethiopia, is located in the far western part of the country. It's out where the mountains, or highlands as they like to call them, have turned back into the Sudanese grasslands. It's flat and hot. Very hot. I had just recently been there with Glen to check it out and make preparations for taking a small Work & Witness team of men to construct a church. I now found myself back in Gambella with the guys and ready to build.

Gambella is best described like the old American Wild West. Its population is mostly made up of two different tribes of Sudanese refugees: the Nuer and the Anuak. Even though both of these tribes are from Sudan and had both fled the dangers of the civil war in their country, they still didn't care much for each other.

The river that divided Gambella also kept the two tribes separated. The Anuaks were on one side, and the Nuer were on the other. On the Nuer side was a vibrant Nazarene church that was always packed out for services. The Anuaks had a site to worship and a lot of attendees but no church building. We were there to build that church for the Anuaks. It would have been nice for both tribes to worship together in one church, but the majority of both sides of town were not Christians and wouldn't take too kindly to have the other tribe walking through their part of town, even if they were fleeing a tidal wave.

The group of guys who were on this team were well experienced and used to rough conditions, and it was a good thing. We were able to secure a so-called motel for the guys. The rooms had ceiling fans that spun so slow, you only knew they were on when you heard them squeak, and that was when the power was working. That was our air-conditioning.

The motel did have a restaurant that basically served only spaghetti…without meat sauce. We just called it white spaghetti. Thank the Lord for the peanut butter we brought with us. When I was there with Glen, I told the guy responsible for delivering the materials from far away Addis Ababa to bring multiple cases of bottled water every time they would bring a load of cinder blocks and secure it somewhere safe. It turned out to be a wise move. There was no access to any type of safe water, and it was hot. Daily temperatures would soar to well over one hundred, and Mr. Sun was doing his best to drive us to our knees. It stayed so consistently hot that some of the guys nicknamed Gambella "the Torch." No one disagreed.

Our buddy Friday had joined us in our endeavor there, and after a few days, we had made some pretty good progress. There were two Anuak women who were helping on the job site. One was probably in her thirties and the other in her forties, but both looked well advanced in years due to the incredibly harsh living conditions. They showed up every day in the same rags for clothes but worked just as hard as everyone else carrying blocks or buckets of concrete. The guys had a deep respect for them and pitched in to purchase and present to them some new dresses on the last day on the job site. You could say some tears were shed.

As we were working one of the days, Stephen showed up with his JESUS Film team and told us that he planned on showing the film that night to the Anuaks. They had gone around announcing it to the local community, and we were all in. We would show it on the site where we were building. After the sun went down and we had polished off another incredible plate of white spaghetti, we headed back to the site for the JESUS Film. Several hundred Anuaks had shown up in anticipation.

Stephen and his guys were set up with the reel-to-reel projector, and after a brief introduction, the first reel was started. It didn't take long to realize that something was wrong. The picture was projecting just fine, but the sound was coming out garbled. Not that I'm fluent in Sudanese Anuak, but it was obvious the sound wasn't working.

Stephen and the guys stopped the film and worked on the sound system and projector then started it back up. It was the same, only the picture but no sound. They tried again. Same result. You could tell people were getting restless. Our team was praying. Here was a great way to reach these people right in front of us, and something or someone was blocking it. Stephen gave it one more try, but it didn't work. They had to make an announcement and apologize. They told them that if they would all come back the next night, they would show it then. They all went home, and we went back to our squeaky fans.

The next day, we were laying blocks on the church, and I saw Stephen and his team under a tree working on the equipment trying to figure out what was going on. He later told us everything was working just fine now, and they were ready for that night. I wondered how many people would come back. The sun went down, we had a belly full of noodles, and we headed back over to the job site for the JESUS Film.

The crowd turned out to be about the same size as the night before. A couple of announcements were made, and the first reel was started. The sound was perfect. But now something was wrong with the picture. It was all blurry on the screen. You couldn't make out anything that was being done, you could only hear them talking. It all had been working perfectly that afternoon. Instead of stopping the film this time to work on the projector, the decision was made to keep it rolling while they tried to tweak it.

Stephen had his flashlight out and was going over everything, trying to find the issue on that EIKI projector. The Anuaks didn't seem to mind. They were listening and understanding what was being said in their own language. With this projector set up, the JESUS Film had four reels to make up the two-hour movie. That means that each reel runs for about thirty minutes as they work their way from beginning to end through the Gospel of Luke.

Stephen worked on that projector through the whole first reel's thirty minutes and was never able to get the picture to come out on the screen correctly. They thought if we kept running the film, we might do damage to the film itself. Once again, the decision was made to call it off. Two nights in a row. It was disappointing but understandable. This was our last shot to show it because Stephen and his team were heading somewhere else the next day.

The crowd was still there when Friday came over to me and said in his Kenyan accent, "Brother Jeff, speak to the people and give an invitation."

I basically responded with, "Are you crazy? We're lucky they haven't stoned us. They've only listened to the first few chapters of Luke in this first reel. A few miracles maybe, but no crucifixion, no resurrection, and you want to give an invitation?"

He said, "Yes, give an invitation to them."

I said, "OK, but I'm going to have to take some time with them. Is that alright?"

"Yes, brother, talk to them."

As I walked up in front of them to take my place next to an interpreter and to grab hold of the microphone, I prayed for the Lord to make this clear to them. I know many times a foreigner can stand up in front of a crowd and ask them to accept or do almost anything, and they will just because he's a foreigner. I don't know why that is the case, but it is. I didn't want that here. I wanted it to be clear to them what it actually meant to accept Christ into their hearts. For the next few minutes, the Lord said something to them through the interpreter.

After only listening to the first few chapters of the Gospel of Luke and a few minutes of explaining what it means to accept Jesus into their lives, over sixty Anuak walked forward to accept that invitation. I wouldn't have believed it if I didn't see it. I honestly thought Friday was crazy, but that's the power of God's Word. A frustrating two nights turned into a celebration.

We finished the Anuak church and worshipped in it that Sunday morning. We saw two ladies present in brand-new dresses. We then traveled across the river and worshipped with the Nuer church later that Sunday. Our plates were full and not with spaghetti this time.

Just several weeks after we returned home from the Torch, we heard that an Anuak had gotten into a skirmish with a native Ethiopian somewhere in the Highlands and allegedly killed him. In reprisal, Ethiopian troops were sent to the Anuak side of Gambella and brutally killed dozens of innocent Anuaks right out in the streets. I've often wondered if any of those dozens were part of the sixty or so who came forward to accept Christ just a few weeks before.

> So then faith comes from hearing, and hearing from the Word of God.
> —Romans 10:17

CHAPTER 15

THE DAY NO ONE WILL FORGET

We had spent the last week and a half with Doc out in the Amazon jungle. After finishing up our projects there, our small team of guys made it by boat to the little jungle town of Nieva to spend the night. We were beginning our long several-day trek to get back to Lima and then home to the USA. We had one more leg of boat travel from Nieva to the mission station up the Marañón River.

After a decent night's rest, we climbed into our open johnboats with our gear and started our eight-hour journey to the mission station. It was a typical morning in the jungle. It was cool with low clouds hanging just over the trees and the river. All that tends to burn off before too long as the Amazon sun makes its appearance for the day.

I never minded these hours-long boat rides in the jungle because they offered some of the most pristine scenery in the world. Yes, it can be a dangerous place to be, but I believe the Amazon jungle is still the most beautiful place on the planet. These boat rides also gave you time to reflect. The Lord had blessed us again. The guys were relatively healthy and had a good trip. We would all be with our families in just a few days.

I also started thinking about another upcoming trip that I had scheduled within a few days of returning home that would send me back to India. I was going back through Harvest Partners again to work with Campus Crusade to do more JESUS Film seminars like I had done the year before. But first, we had to get out of the jungle and get home.

We were making our way up the Marañón. The sun had come out and was doing his thing, but up ahead, I noticed what looked like one of those random passing jungle rain storms that pop up. It was hanging over the river ahead of us. I thought, *Great. I'm really not in the mood to get soaked today.* So I decided to try and protect my gear bag from the rain by putting it behind my legs. Then I closed my legs over it as I sat on the metal bench.

I watched as we crept closer to the distinct wall of water falling from the sky. As we hit it, I pulled my hat down tighter and bent over my exposed thighs to ride it out. It was pouring, but because of the way I was sitting combined with the forward motion of the boat, I was staying relatively dry. The passing rain burst soon moved on, and I was pretty impressed with myself for how dry I stayed.

That's when I felt a flow of cold water go right down the inside of the back of my pants as I sat there. I turned to see Doc sitting on the bench right behind me laughing. He had pulled out his rain poncho and put it on when he saw the rain coming. He then proceeded to collect a huge puddle of the cool liquid on the front of his poncho as he watched my efforts to stay dry. At the right time, he decided to empty his poncho's contents down the back of my pants and soaked me. Oh well, I'm glad I made his day. I'll make sure not to sit in front of Doc in the future.

We eventually made it to the banks of the mission station that afternoon and began unloading our gear. Doc's wife, Addie, would be there and always made us a feast as we would be on our way out of the jungle. A lot of times, it would be hard to eat all she would make for us, after adjusting ourselves to the local jungle cuisine we had been consuming for several days. But I could always make room for her fresh mango pie.

We made our way up the river bank and started heading to the bunkhouse to drop off our gear for the night. We were met by Addie. Instead of her normal warm "Welcome back," she was a bit hysterical, and we knew something was wrong. She kept saying, "We've been attacked, and over fifty thousand are dead!" This day was September 11, 2001.

Although the preliminary numbers were off, the message was correct, and we heard about it in the Amazon jungle the same day it happened. We didn't have many details, but we did have concerns for our families back in the States. Doc got his ham radio going and was able to connect with a friend in Ohio who could then patch each of us through by phone to our wives one by one. Everyone felt a bit more relieved after speaking with our families. It seemed like that dangerous jungle was now safer than the USA.

Of course, we learned that all the airports had been shut down with no signs of reopening, which added a new dynamic to our situation. We discussed it as a group and decided to continue to travel, as normal, toward Lima and see what the situation would be when we got there. If the airports were still closed at that point, at least we would be close to one when they reopened. This would give us a hotel to hang out in at least.

We still had a few days' travel to get us to that scenario. I had another situation as well. I was supposed to be going to India in a few days after getting back. That trip was now in serious jeopardy. When I had the chance to speak with Angie, she told me that the travel agent had contacted her to tell her that because of the situation, we could return the tickets for India within the next couple of days for a full refund or risk losing all the ticket money if things stayed status quo. I told Angie to wait another day until our group made it over the Andes and into the city of Chiclayo, and then I would find a way to call her and let her know.

Once we reached Chiclayo, nothing had changed. The airports were still shut down even after much prayer. I found a place where I could call Angie and told her where we were and that we were doing well. Then she asked about the tickets to India. I told her, "At this point, I don't even know if I can get home, I guess you should take the tickets back to the travel agent. At least we'll get the money back."

That was a disappointing decision to make. I knew how effective those JESUS Film seminars had been the previous year on the east coast of India, and I was looking forward to training thousands of more leaders in another part of India. But right now, the world was broken. I guess the Lord had other plans. Angie took the tickets to the travel agent the next day and told her to return them.

The guys and I finally made it to Lima. The hotels near the airport were packed with people whose flights had been canceled and were put on stand-by if or when the airports would reopen. We thought we would be joining them, but when we arrived, the airports opened up. We weren't going to be put on standby or wait at all because our originally scheduled flight from Lima to Atlanta was to be the very first international flight from Peru to the USA, and we had tickets for it. Thank you, Lord!

The flight crew who had flown that plane to Lima stayed onboard as passengers on the way back to Atlanta. Every other would be empty seat was filled with someone who had been waiting for days to get back to the States. That was a very full flight. When we landed in Atlanta, we were the only plane in the international section of that normally very busy airport. The only other people walking around were armed military. It was quite strange to see this in America.

The guys split up in Atlanta to catch their respective flights back to Virginia. Some were headed to Roanoke and some others elsewhere, and three of us were to fly to Richmond. We said our goodbyes and went to our gates. When we got on our flight to Richmond, we were the only passengers on the plane. We had the plane to ourselves. That would never happen again. We were just overjoyed to get home to our families.

I was happy and thankful for another successful trip with Doc and being able to help him in his ministry in Peru. I was also happy and thankful for quite an interesting and safe journey back home to my family. But I had to admit that there was something that just kept gnawing at me for having to cancel my trip to India. I tried putting it out of my head. What choice did I have at the time? It seemed like God shut the door…but my spirit wouldn't let it go.

> He who dwells in the secret place of the Most High shall abide under the shadow of the Almighty. I will say of the Lord, "He is my Refuge and my Fortress; my God, in Him I will trust." Surely He shall deliver you from the snare of the fowler and from the perilous pestilence. He shall cover you with His feathers, and under His wings you shall take refuge.
> —Psalm 91:1–4A

CHAPTER 16

WELL, WHAT NOW?

It was great to be home again. I was able to spend some time with Angie and the girls and fill them in on what had happened in the jungle on our recent trip with Doc. It seemed like I was going to have more time than expected since we returned my tickets to India. I would have already been preparing for that trip since it was scheduled in just a few days.

As happy as I was to be spending quality time with the family, there was still this gnawing in my spirit that I should be going to India. I tried to dismiss it as nonsense. Obviously the Lord shut that door, and I needed to move on. Right? But I couldn't stop thinking about it.

I couldn't sleep much because of this obsession. The notion to go wouldn't leave me alone. I finally had a conversation with God that went something like this: "Lord, I don't know if You're trying to tell me something or if I'm just going crazy. You know I was willing to go to India for You and would still go but it seemed so obvious that You shut that door. The world is on edge, I now have no tickets and probably couldn't get any in this short of a time span anyway, but the biggest obstacle is a wife who just went through the emotional roller coaster of 9/11 while I was in a different country. I can't even bring this subject up to her. She'll think I'm nuts if she doesn't throttle me first for even bringing the subject up. I'll check into going, Lord, but you're gonna have to tell her first." I left it at that. I wasn't going to say anything. I figured that now maybe I could get some peace about the situation and some sleep.

You can imagine my shock when Angie came to me the next morning and said, "I couldn't sleep much last night, and I prayed about it, and well…I think you should go to India." I was so stunned that I think I forgot to breathe until she said it again. "I think you should go to India." She would tell me later that she was afraid to tell me because she was the one who had turned the tickets in to the travel agent, and now the trip seemed impossible. So while I was having a conversation with God, He was having one with Angie. Now what do we do?

Angie and I were on the same page and decided that we would go in person and talk to our travel agent. It was extremely short notice to try to book an international flight. One might say impossible. And we knew that even if, by some miracle, we were able to secure new tickets, they would probably be incredibly expensive compared to the ones I had booked well in advance. We put it in the Lord's hands to work it out.

Angie and I drove to the travel agency and found our agent sitting behind her desk. We sat there and began to tell our saga to her. We said we figured this warranted a personal visit instead of trying to explain all this "crazy talk" over a phone call. She sat there patiently.

Finally we got to the part about turning in the old tickets to her so she could return them for a refund. We said, "We know it's going to be expensive, but is there any possibility of buying new tickets with this short notice?" She sat there in silence for a moment. Then this strange look came over her face as she mumbled, "Those tickets, those tickets..." She spun around in her office chair and began to shuffle through stacks of loose papers on top of a low bookshelf that was behind her desk against the wall.

As she did this, her mumbling became louder and clearer. "Those tickets..." Amid a sea of loose papers, she pulled out a ticket packet, and as she spun her chair back around to face us, she exclaimed, "I forgot to return your tickets for a refund...here they are." And just like that, I had my original tickets handed right back to me. Angie and I just sat there and looked at each other and smiled.

I felt like thanking the travel agent for her dereliction of duty, but there was no way for that to come out right. So I just said, "Thanks," and left, smiling in unbelief all the way home. Now Angie was excited about the trip too. I guess God had a plan and wanted both of us involved in it. I was to leave in just a couple of days.

The trip was scheduled to last about three weeks. I didn't know where I was going in India once I got there, but I knew there would be a lot of traveling, so I wanted to pack light. I was able to get everything I needed into one small carry-on bag. I figured this would simplify things. Due to the debacle of having to change airports in Mumbai at 2:00 a.m. the year before, I made sure that I was securely booked all the way to Bangalore this time. I never wanted to endure that experience of being left out on my own in a major foreign city again.

On September 20, I left for Dulles Airport just outside of Washington, DC, with my old "new" tickets in hand and an anticipation of being a part of what God had planned. I walked into Dulles and looked for the check-in desk of the airline that would be my home for the next seventeen-plus hours of flying time. As I was looking, the loudspeakers in the airport came on and said, "Jeff Jackson, you have a phone call." (This was before the cell phone craze.)

Surely that can't be me, I thought. In an airport of this size, there must be another, more important Jeff Jackson walking around. Then

I heard it again, "Jeff Jackson, you have a phone call. Report to the main desk." I figured I better check it out.

When I got to the main desk and told them that I was Jeff Jackson, they handed the phone to me. I said, "Hello," wondering who in the world would be calling me at Dulles Airport. It was my travel agent of all people. She said, "I know you're ready to go, but I wanted to tell you about the part of the world you're traveling to. All the American-based airlines have just announced they have canceled all flights going to that area of the world for security reasons. But since you booked with an Indian airline, they are still flying there because it's their country." She continued, "I was concerned for your safety and thought you needed to know this as an American heading over there. I don't know if you still want to go or not since this news came out, but I thought you should know. I know you'll make the right decision."

I said, "Thank you for your concern and for letting me know," and we said our goodbyes.

Now what do I do? I hadn't checked in yet, and I only had one carry-on bag. I could easily walk out the doors and go home. I had to go somewhere and pray about this. And of course, there's no better place to pray than the public restroom of an international airport. I made my way into the men's room, took a stall, and shut the door.

I started by saying, "Lord, what do *You* want me to..." and before I could finish my thought, I strongly and distinctively felt God's response as follows: "Have I not commanded you? Be strong and of good courage; do not be afraid, nor dismayed, for the Lord your God is with you wherever you go." A sense of absolute peace washed over me, and I had my answer. I left the stall, washed my hands (just because it was a public restroom), and made my way to check-in.

Later as I made my way to the gate, I started thinking about what the travel agent had said to me about all the American-based airlines canceling all their flights like that. That's when it dawned on me that in all of my travels up to this point, I had always traveled with American-based airlines. This was the very first time I had booked with a foreign airline of any kind. Truly God had a plan He wanted accomplished. It was becoming clearer that I was just along for the ride.

> Have I not commanded you? Be strong and of good courage; Do not be afraid, nor be dismayed, for the Lord your God is with you wherever you go.
> —Joshua 1:9

CHAPTER 17

JUST TAKE A TAXI

After over seventeen hours of flight time with a kid kicking the back of my seat for most of the way, I was looking forward to getting off the plane in Bangalore, India. It would be nice to get to the Campus Crusade for Christ Center and see some old friends and get a little rest before my next assignment started. It was all worked out that someone from Campus Crusade would pick me up outside the airport doors because nontravelers weren't allowed inside this particular airport.

I grabbed my carry-on bag and headed out the doors. Once I got outside, I was greeted by about eighty eager taxi drivers all wanting my business. I continuously waved them off while I looked for my ride that should be there. I couldn't find my contact anywhere.

Meanwhile, the taxi drivers were relentless. After about thirty minutes of this, I figured I better call someone. I pulled out my information folder and scanned it for a phone number. I had names but no numbers of any kind.

I thought about calling home to see if I could get Angie to find a number somewhere in my office. That's when I realized that I wasn't allowed back into the airport since I had gone outside. This was before the cell phone craze. I said, "OK, plan B." I started looking at my information for the address of Campus Crusade, but of course, I didn't have that either. All I had was eighty taxi drivers. I thought, *Here we go again.* I'm gonna have to trust one of these guys to get me to my destination without disappearing down some back alley.

After a quick prayer, I cleared my throat and loudly asked my eighty new friends if anyone knew how to get to the Campus Crusade for Christ Campus. I got eighty affirmatives. I knew that wasn't right. So based on the selection process I had just used the year before in Mumbai, I looked for the smallest, skinniest driver there and said, "Let's go." As we walked toward his taxi, I asked him again, "Are you sure you know where Campus Crusade is?" He assured me that he did.

I climbed into the back seat, and we left the airport. We started driving down the crowded streets, and I started wondering what happened to my contacts and why they never showed. I also thanked the Lord that it wasn't 2:00 a.m. like the last time I had to flag a taxi but was closer to 7:00 a.m. and the sun was up.

As my driver continued to drive and make turns here and there, I was beginning to think, *I don't remember it taking this long last year to get to Campus Crusade.* I asked my driver if he was alright and knew where he was going. He responded with just a painful look on his face. That's when it was confirmed to me that he had no idea where Campus Crusade was, and we were just driving around the city.

I said, "Is there anyone you could call to find out where it is?"

He said, "Yes." And we looked for a public phone. We stopped a few minutes later, and he got out to make a phone call. I offered a few more prayers for the situation. He came back to the taxi with his head down. Apparently no one knew where Campus Crusade was located.

I said, "OK, Let's just start driving." I don't know what my thinking was. I guess I thought, *We're not going to find it sitting here.* At the time, the city of Bangalore was a bit smaller than New York City with a population of just under seven million people. For India, it wasn't one of their bigger cities, but to this boy from rural Virginia, it was big enough. This particular morning it was huge.

We continued to drive and make turns, left and right, for about another thirty minutes. Then we made a left turn onto a street that had a distinctive arc to it that went to the right. It looked strangely familiar to me. I said, "Go up here and take a right." We did and then made another turn, and lo and behold, there was the entrance gate to Campus Crusade for Christ. The painful look that had been on my driver's face was all smiles…and so was mine.

I had only been in this city one time and briefly the year before, and yet the Lord installed some sort of supernatural recall and directed my tiny driver and me to literally find a needle in a haystack. I think we'd still be driving around Bangalore today if God hadn't intervened. I wonder sometimes if He doesn't just roll His eyes at us when we do something like forget to bring phone numbers and addresses on an international trip. That won't happen again.

I thanked the Lord and my driver as I sent him on his way. Who knows if he ever made it back to the airport. I was let through the gates and began walking across the grounds. It was unusually quiet. It was still fairly early in the morning, but usually someone would be out somewhere. I found the residence of my contact and knocked on his door. After some delay, I knocked again. Finally I heard the unlatching of the locks, and the door opened. There was my contact squinting in the morning light.

I had obviously woken him up. Before I could say anything, his eyes opened up and he said, "What are you doing here?"

I said, "I'm supposed to be here according to the schedule we had."

He said, "Yes, I know, but we didn't think anyone was coming." I gave him a few minutes to get dressed and come out so we could figure out what was going on.

We sat down to discuss the situation. He told me that there were supposed to be eight of us showing up. We were to be set out in pairs around India to lead seminars, similar to last year. Apparently some backed out, and others had their American-based airline flights canceled. I was the only one who showed up. He figured I wasn't coming either and didn't bother to go to the airport to pick me up. He apologized for that, and I told him the equivalent of, "No problem at all, and by the way, you have a lovely city." I wasn't going to let him know what my heart rate had been doing the last couple of hours.

He had been in the process of canceling the seminars around India but hadn't canceled them all just yet. There was an area in South West India where he wanted to send me. After going through all the details, he told me that I would have different handlers as I traveled through different areas of their responsibility. They would pass me off to the next guys when I finished the seminars where they were from.

Then he told me that they had hired me a driver and that he would be with me for the entire three weeks. I thought, *Great, at least I'm not going to have to be flying around or taking trains again.*

Then he informed me, "He's a Muslim from Saudi Arabia, and we wanted to expose him to the Gospel." This was September 22, 2001. I first looked to see if he was kidding. Surely he must be kidding. When I realized he was serious, my first thought was, *Are you nuts putting an American in the hands of a Muslim right now? And from Saudi Arabia no less.* I only thought it and didn't say it out loud to my host, but man, was I thinking it.

I agreed with the situation, finalized some details, tried to get some rest, and prepared myself for a new adventure that would start the next day. I prayed that night, "Lord, I don't know what You're up to, but help me to be useful."

> You shall seek them and not find them,
> those who contended with you. Those who war
> against you shall be as nothing, as a nonexistent

thing. For I, the Lord your God, will hold your right hand, saying
    To you, "Fear not, I will help you."
—Isaiah 41:12–13

CHAPTER 18

THE LAND OF COCONUTS

As we packed up our vehicle, we were given several cases of a brand-new evangelistic tool to take with us. It was called an Evangecube. It was about the size of the old Rubik's cube and was covered with several pictures that showed the basic Gospel story. It would unfold and fold back up in different ways like some sort of cubic origami. There were also no words printed on it so it could be used in any language. You would just quote verses that went along with the pictures being displayed that laid out the plan of salvation.

They gave us enough Evangecubes to get started with the first few seminars so that every participant would receive one as well as a copy of the JESUS Film in their own language. They asked me to train the attendees in how to use these Evangecubes somewhere in the JESUS Film trainings. I had never seen one of these cubes before, but it looked simple enough and agreed with the plan.

I was introduced to my Saudi driver. We'll call him Sam.[3] Sam seemed pleasant enough and could speak English, which was a plus. But to be honest, I kept my guard up just a bit. Sam climbed behind the wheel, a couple of Indians climbed into the back seat, and I rode shotgun. We were off to the Indian state of Kerala, located in the southwest section of India.

Kerala means "the land of the coconuts" in the local language, and it lived up to its reputation. It was beautiful, green, and lush. As we traveled along, I noticed on the seat between Sam and me was a small rolled-up rug. I didn't ask what it was because I thought it might be Sam's Muslim prayer rug. My suspicions were confirmed when out of the blue, with no warning, Sam pulled the vehicle over with a screeching halt. He grabbed the small rug and got out of the vehicle without a word and walked off to a private spot somewhere to do his Muslim prayers toward Mecca, leaving the three of us in the vehicle. The first few times he did this surprised me, but I soon got used to it.

We made it to our first seminar, and everything went as planned. I was able to train hundreds of attendees on the strategies of using the JESUS Film and gave my first training on the Evangecube. While I stood up front and looked over the crowd, I could see out the back and noticed that Sam stayed out there close to our vehicle and not paying much attention to anything being said. This soon changed after a couple more of these sessions.

I don't know if Sam just wanted to get out of the sun or if he had started listening to what was being said. Maybe he was beginning to lower his guard just a bit as we were getting more and more acquainted with each other. One thing I did notice was when I was training several hundred people at a time on how to use the Evangecube that it was very difficult for everyone to see this small cube in my hands up on stage. That's when I asked Sam if he wanted

---

[3] Sam—not the driver's real name but is used for his protection.

to assist me with this portion of the seminar. I figured all he could say was "No," but he agreed.

So I would put Sam, armed with his own Evangecube, about halfway down the center aisle. As I told the Gospel story and displayed how the cube worked to the front half of the crowd, there was Sam listening and synchronizing with me in displaying how it worked to the back half of the crowd. He seemed happy to be involved in the process. But I knew every time we did this, Sam was being exposed to the fact that Jesus Christ came to die for him. Sometimes it was several times a day.

We were making our way through the land of the coconuts one seminar at a time when I spied a public phone outfit and thought that maybe I should try to call home and let Angie know what's going on and where I am. Typically I wouldn't go out of my way to call home on a trip. Angie and I had made an agreement that "No news is good news." In those days, it was often hard to find a phone in the places I found myself in. But with the world situation, maybe this might be a good time to check in.

Despite the time difference of me being in the next day, it was a convenient time to try to reach her. She picked up the phone right away. After letting her know that I was still alive, she asked me for an update because everyone at church had been hounding her for information. I said, "OK, tell them I was in a den in Bombay."

She said, "Oh wait, let me get something to write with… OK, go ahead. You were in a den in Bombay?"

I said, "Yep, and I had a slack jaw and not much to say."

She said, "Slack jaw?"

"Yep," I said.

She said, "What's a slack…wait a minute. Isn't that a song?"[4]

"Yep."

We worked all that out, had a good laugh, and then I gave her a real update of what the Lord had been doing. After that, I told her, "Tomorrow is beautiful." That was something I always told her whenever I happened to be in the next day's time zone and had a

---

[4] Men at Work—"Down Under."

chance to talk with her. We were soon back on the road and had been going for a couple of weeks at this point.

Every few days or so, the guys in the back seat would change, but Sam and I were always up front. He couldn't understand anything being said in the back seat any more than I could, but there was always a constant chatter of the Malayalam language flying around inside the vehicle. One time during a particularly long stretch of backseat conversing, Sam and I looked at each other, and I said to him in a hushed tone, "Blah blah blah blah blah blah." He started laughing so hard, I became concerned that he might drive us off the road.

It was right after that moment that it hit me: "Lord, what in the world am I doing here? An American in the middle of nowhere in India with Indians in the back seat, a Muslim driver, and a world on the brink of who knows what?" You couldn't script this up. Sam was still giggling. I just looked out the side window and smiled. I felt like the Lord was probably smiling too.

The seminars continued to click off successfully, and we were nearing the end of the trip. After one of those events, four of us climbed into the vehicle and had a several-hour drive in front of us. I noticed Sam was pretty quiet as we started out. He seemed to be in deep thought. Suddenly, out of the blue, he said, "You know, I don't believe Jesus actually died on the cross." It was obvious that he had been pondering this thought for a while.

Sam had heard the Gospel every day and even helped in presenting it. The Holy Spirit was working on him, but he showed a lot of courage to actually say something about it. For the next hour or so, my friends in the back seat and I explained to Sam, as plainly as we could, that Jesus had to die on the cross, or there would be no price paid for our sins. He listened as he drove. He would make an occasional comment or offer his opinion on the matter, but we answered everything he brought up. Sam was quiet the rest of that leg, and I could tell the Lord was working on him.

In a few days, we finished up our assignment, and it was time for me to go back to the States. The trip was a huge success. In the coming weeks, I would end up receiving letters from pastors and leaders I didn't know, who had been in those large seminar crowds. I even got pictures of baptisms that took place, out of the results of using the tools we brought them. Overall, it was a cause for celebration looking back at it. I could see why God wanted me to go on this trip no matter what, and why the devil fought it.

As far as Sam goes, he never accepted Christ as his Savior while I was with him, although the opportunity was presented to him. He had hoped to be able to return to Saudi Arabia someday after he had saved up some money. I don't know if he ever did. What dawned on me through this whole experience was that God doesn't care what state of upheaval the world may be in, He is still in control and will get His purpose accomplished even when we might think it's crazy. And even though He reached the masses in southwest India, at the same time, He cared enough to reach out and expose His love to one lonely foreigner and offer forgiveness to him if he would only accept it. I hope to one day see Sam again in the presence of the One Who died for him.

> Jesus said to him, "I Am the Way, the Truth, and the Life. No one comes to the Father except through me."
> —John 14:6

CHAPTER 19

THE RAID ON ENTEBBE

Dave and I had two exciting and successful trips to Khartoum, Sudan, and were able to deliver four sets of JESUS Film equipment into the hands of our contacts there. But there was a need for more. We feel like we had about worn out our welcome with the authorities in the north. It was a miracle to be able to get visas the first time to get in, but twice was totally unheard of, and a third may be pushing it a bit. We also knew that we had been followed off and on during our stay.

The next equipment was needed more in the southern part of the country, so we decided to take a different approach. Uganda is the country that borders Southern Sudan to its south. We had contacts there. If we could get JESUS Film equipment into Uganda, our Southern Sudanese contacts could take it from us and across the border into South Sudan.

Dave and I met up at Dulles Airport near Washington, DC, and approached the ticket counter to check in and pay the fees to get all the extra baggage checked in all the way to Entebbe, Uganda. And once again, we had a pile of luggage. As Dave was talking with the agent at the counter, I noticed the man checking in at the counter to our immediate right had a bunch of luggage as well. He wasn't going to Entebbe. I kept moving our bags and tried to keep them separated from his bags. But somehow they kept mingling with ours despite my best efforts. So again I tried to slide our bags over close to us. The last thing I wanted to do was to lose a bag and have it shipped to who knows where.

We finally got all the details taken care of, and one by one, we passed our bags through the opening to be tagged and taken by the agents at the counter. When we finished, our neighbor to the right finished as well. Dave and I were ready to go. We had never been to Uganda before. Neither one of us knew what to expect or how it was going to be to try and get bags of electronic film equipment through customs without being seen. But we had both done this enough by now to know that we weren't alone, and God always has a plan even if He never told us what it was ahead of time. Dave and I prayed on the way that God would once again make a way to get His Word to His people.

I had heard the stories about Uganda when I was young. They had an infamous ruler back then named Edi Amin. One time, there had been a highjacked Israeli jetliner at Entebbe where Israel had sent commandos there to rescue their people on a daring mission. It became known as the Raid on Entebbe. I was hoping our arrival would be a bit less dramatic.

Our plane arrived pretty late at night to Entebbe. We went through the immigration process with the rest of the passengers without a problem. We then headed to baggage claim together to collect our bags and get through customs. When we entered the room where the baggage carousel was, I began to try to look ahead to see what might be in store for us at customs. I didn't like what I saw.

Everyone was to pick up their luggage and be escorted into an adjoining room that was full of empty tables. We were to put all our luggage on those tables to be personally hand-searched by the Ugandan officials. There was no way around it…so I thought.

The carousel began to move, and bags began to come out on it. People began to pick off their bags and head right into the search room. Our bags began to come out one by one sprinkled in with all the others. Dave and I began to pile up our bags as we waited for all of them to appear. And we waited and waited.

I kept looking through the glass walls as the rest of our fellow passengers had all of their luggage opened up on the inspection tables and being rifled through like a dog burying a bone. I thought, *They're gonna love us*. We kept waiting for our last bag to appear so we could join the fun next door, but it just wasn't coming.

After a while, Dave and I were the only two left in the carousel room. Our last bag had not shown up yet, and most of the other passengers were done and gone. As the carousel kept going around, there was one large bag on it, but it wasn't ours. Finally the carousel stopped, and we realized we were missing a bag of equipment, and someone else had left a bag on the carousel. We were going to have to file a missing bag report.

We grabbed the rest of our bags and headed to the window to explain what happened and to describe what our missing bag looked like. As the lady behind the glass was writing down our information, I glanced back at the one lone bag sitting on the now silent carousel. My mind went back to the check-in desk at Dulles Airport where our pile of bags kept comingling with our neighbor's pile of bags. Could it be that one of our bags went with him, and I'm now looking at one of his bags in front of me in Uganda?

The process to fill out the missing bag report took forever but was now complete. It was early morning at this point. As Dave and I began to gather up our bags, there were no guards left in the area. The lights were turned off in the search room, and I looked back to see one lonely bag still sitting on the carousel. We knew where the exit was and wasted no time walking right out to our waiting contacts without having one of our bags inspected. The "old lost baggage" option didn't occur to Dave and me, but the Lord had our backs again.

We found out later that our suspicions were correct. Our one missing bag had gone with our check-in neighbor to Lagos, Nigeria, and his missing bag was sent with us to Uganda. We headed to Kampala to get some rest. That afternoon, we were at the office in Kampala when a delivery showed up from the airport in Entebbe. It was our missing bag of equipment. It had come in on a morning flight from Lagos and was immediately driven to the address we had left with them at the airport. It was never inspected either.

Once again, the Lord accomplished His purpose in His own way. That made two more complete sets of JESUS Film equipment safely headed for use in Sudan to reach those who had never had the opportunity to hear or see Jesus before.

> Yours, O Lord, is the greatness, the power and the glory, the victory and the majesty; For all that is in heaven and in earth is Yours; Yours is the kingdom, O Lord, and You are exalted as Head over all.
> —1 Chronicles 29:11

CHAPTER 20

WHERE DID ALL THE WITCH DOCTORS GO?

When a Baptist friend, who has no problem sacrificing to help build numerous Nazarene churches around the globe, asks if you could help out on a project he's working on, it is an honor to say "Yes." Dave and I were headed to the Amazon jungle again, but this time to the Orinoco region of Venezuela.

We had to obtain permission from the Venezuelan authorities to go where not many had been before. Once we had that, we flew from Caracas to the last town that had an airport on the border of Venezuela and Colombia. From there, we loaded up on Mission Aviation planes. Those are the real small ones where everyone is sitting with the pilot and they weigh every item to disburse the weight evenly around the plane so it can take off and stay in the air. I have to admit, I've never been a fan of traveling by these means, but it was the only way to get to these remote jungle villages.

Once we got airborne and were headed deep into the Amazon, we saw nothing but lush jungle and rivers as far as we could see. After a couple of hours of flying and passing a few impressive waterfalls, we were coming in for a landing in our target village called Coshiwateli, or Cosh as the locals call it. We circled over the village to let them know we were coming in and to make sure they cleared any grazing animals that might be on the grass runway.

As we made our approach, I noticed in the river just at the end of the runway, a plane just like ours submerged on the bottom. I found out later, they had too much weight in the back of the plane as they tried to take off from Cosh, and it crashed into the river almost immediately. I told you—not a fan.

But we landed without incident, unloaded our gear, and settled into our homes for the next few days. We were staying with one of the missionary families who was living in this village. There were various projects that needed to be worked on around the village. The main project for us was to complete a medical building or clinic in the center of the village. We were able to do this in a couple of days and proceeded to work on some other projects as well. We even put a cement floor in the village pastor's house. He just happened to be the former witch doctor for the village.

We were invited to a wedding feast in the village that consisted of various pots of prized game brought back by a village hunting party. After sampling the different species presented, I made a note of when offered the choice between monkey and jungle rat...always go with the jungle rat.

Once we had our work done, we were given an opportunity to travel down the rivers to other villages to show the JESUS Film and minister to the people. It was an opportunity of a lifetime. The Indian tribe in this part of the Amazon is called the Yanomamö. Their fierceness and savagery is well known in the books written about them. Although Cosh had settled down for the most part, the villages we were about to encounter were still a generation or two behind them in their civilized evolution. The villages were still run and controlled by the local witch doctors.

Early in the morning, we loaded up several large dugout canoes with supplies for the trip. I was even handed a plastic pouch of hard-boiled eggs in case we got hungry. We climbed aboard and started downriver. Before we could really settle in, we were pulling over to a village that was very close to Cosh. The missionaries wanted to talk to the leader there. The leader's name was Hot, and he also happened to be the witch doctor for that village.

Judging by Hot's reaction to us, I could tell he didn't expect us. In fact, he looked terrified. As the missionaries talked with him, he never turned his back to us or took his eyes off us. They were just catching him up on local news, so it wasn't long before we were back in the canoes and on our way. The missionaries told us they have witnessed to Hot repeatedly, but he always resisted making a decision for Christ.

Minutes turned into hours as we navigated our way through the jungle on the river. The coolness of the morning was now gone. Sitting in our canoe, I watched as pairs of macaws flew overhead using the open river, heading to destinations unknown to me. We finally came to another Yanomamö village. When we asked to see the witch doctor to announce our arrival, we were informed that he had just left and gone out into the jungle.

So we stayed for a while and talked with the villagers. When we finished, we loaded up again and continued on in the heat of the afternoon. About midafternoon, I happened to be looking behind me in the canoe and saw that plastic pouch of hard-boiled eggs sitting on top of the other supplies in the blazing jungle sun. There was no way to reach them, and I'm sure at this point, the damage was already done. I made a mental note: "Stay away from the eggs."

We soon pulled up to another village only to discover that their witch doctor had just run off into the jungle right before we got there. I thought that was strange, but we stayed and visited for a while before moving on again. We finally got to the village that we would be calling home for the night and unpacked our gear. When our food supplies were laid out on a table, I spied that pouch of eggs.

I told Dave to stay away from them as I picked up the pouch and set it off to the side away from the food.

We showed the JESUS Film that night in that tiny village with little results. But at least the Gospel was proclaimed. The next morning, we started to take our supplies to the canoes. That's when I noticed that someone had found that pouch of eggs and eaten all of them. All I could say to myself was, "Oh my." We continued down the winding river basically repeating what we had done the day before.

It didn't take long to discover who had eaten the bad eggs as our Indian guides had to frequently pull the canoes to the shoreline and run off into the jungle to relieve some intestinal distress. At least they were laughing at each other about it. On one of these pit stops, I got out to stretch my legs on the shoreline. I took a few strides down the sandy shore and happened to look down to see very large and very fresh jaguar prints in the sand.

He must have gotten himself a drink from the river and was probably still within earshot if not eyeshot. I quickly slid back into the canoe, and our guide announced to his buddy in the jungle that he may want to hurry up. He made it back without incident. As we stopped at the different villages that day, just about every one was absent of a recently vacating witch doctor. But we had a good time visiting with the villagers and listened to their stories as they listened to ours.

We traveled on until the sun was starting to go down. That night, we shared some sort of bony bird over an open flame before hanging up our hammocks from the trees just off the river and retire for a few hours. I never could sleep well in a hammock because I roll too much. But even if I could, I'm not sure I would have on this night knowing I was swinging there like low-hanging fruit in the middle of the Amazon. Thankfully we were all accounted for the next morning, and our journey continued.

To be a part of this voyage was incredible. The Lord blessed us with safety and only some minor intestinal distress for a few. We had the chance to pray for different villagers. One lady we prayed for was suffering from a recent snake bite. But what was still puzzling was the sudden vanishing of multiple witch doctors in so many villages. We discovered the solution to this mystery.

In these villages, the witch doctor or shaman has the power. At some point, they look for a young man who may have the potential to become the next witch doctor. They'll take this young man and put him through an initiation. This involves almost starving him to death and blowing powerful drugs up his nose. This opens the initiate to the spirit world where they are encouraged to talk to and "collect" different spirits to live in their heart.

These spirits will appear to them in familiar animal forms and be able to talk to the young witch doctor just like you and I talk with each other. As the witch doctor progresses in his craft, he tries to collect more spirits, and he becomes more powerful…or he thinks he becomes more powerful. Actually, it's the spirits who are controlling him. And these spirits tell the witch doctors that if they ever try to throw them away or get rid of them, the witch doctor will die.

Of course, these spirits are demons disguising themselves as helpful or powerful entities. You can only imagine the numerous cultures throughout the jungle they have kept in incredible bondage.

These spirits also preach to the witch doctors that the enemy spirit is the great spirit of light who lives above and takes children when they die to eat their souls. They are obviously misrepresenting Almighty God to keep their sham going.

The spirit world for these jungle dwellers is much more real than the physical world that's around them. That's hard for us to understand. But these witch doctors have the ability to look into each other's chests and see what type of spirits are living within the one who stands before them. They also can look at a Christian and see the "enemy" spirit of light living inside of them. That's why Hot was so terrified when we stepped into his village. That's also why so many witch doctors took off right before we arrived as their spirits were urging them to get out of the village because the enemy spirit was coming.

It's a strange feeling to understand this reality, and yet it's also comforting to know the God of the universe lives inside you and the enemy knows it. We really are spiritual beings going through a physical experience here on earth and not physical beings with an occasional spiritual experience. If only we could truly grasp that truth. Several months after we left Cosh, we heard that Hot had finally accepted the Lord.

> You are of God, little children, and have overcome them, because He Who is in you is greater than he who is in the world.
> —1 John 4:4

CHAPTER 21

INTO THE MOUTH OF THE DRAGON

For years, I had been following and supporting an organization whose main purpose for existing is to get Bibles and biblical materials into the hands of believers in countries where the material is either unavailable or illegal to possess. After checking with them to see if they needed any help, an opportunity came up to work with them to get Bibles to underground churches located within mainland China.

Angie and I prayed about it and felt like this is where the Lord was leading us at this time. I reached out to them, received my instructions, booked my flights, and was on my way. I was to land somewhere off the coast of the mainland and be picked up by a team leader from Brazil. Everything went smoothly, and he took me to an apartment where I met the rest of the small group whom I would be working with for the next week or so.

There was a woman from Canada, a man from Australia, a woman from the Netherlands, a brother and sister from Idaho, a man from Denmark, our host leader from Brazil, and me from Virginia. It was pretty cool to see the global family of God come together to help another part of the family who needed it. We would have a meeting in the mornings with our host leader to get our assignment for that day, pick up the materials for that particular day, and then head for the mainland.

Part of the strategy was to split up as we traveled and go through immigration and customs on our own, just in case one of us would get stopped. That way, they wouldn't get the whole group and take all of the materials. Then once we were all on the mainland side, there would be a designated place to meet and regroup and then travel together to our ultimate destination for that day.

Every day was different, and we took turns in assignments as a group, including being the leader of the day. One day, we even went to the local airport on the mainland and flew to Beijing, met our contact at the airport there, and handed off half a dozen luggage carts full of suitcases of Bibles. He and his associates promptly took the loaded carts out the doors and into a waiting open trunk of a running car.

Well one of the days, my turn came up to lead the team. In our meeting that morning, our task was laid out before us. We were to get on the mainland individually with suitcases of Bibles, regroup at a designated location, travel to the train station, get tickets and travel to a large Chinese city, get off and get to that city's subway system, get tickets and navigate that system to a particular stop, get off and walk the rest of the way down the streets and back alleys to a particular underground church, hand off these Bibles to them, and then get back out before dark. And of course, nothing is in English. All I could think of was not to become a headline on the international news that evening.

If I had known the day before that this was going to be the assignment that I was in charge of, I probably wouldn't have slept too well. I guess that's why they never told you in advance. We split up and left for the mainland with our suitcases of Bibles. As I approached the immigration window, I could see some of the rest of the team spread out within the hundreds of people picking from the twenty to thirty lines to go and have their passports checked.

It was my turn in my line, and I stepped up, slid my suitcase up next to my feet, and handed my passport through the little hole in the window to the uniformed guard on the other side. She looked at my passport and then looked up at me. She repeated that process a few more times before turning and calling out a higher-ranking official who was somewhere in the darkened room behind her.

Up stepped a 4'6", 98 lb., fully uniformed female pillar of "all business" who was handed my passport with a comment in Chinese from the guard at the window. This official began the same process of looking down at my passport and up at my face. I smiled as she did this…she didn't. Without a word in English or the local dialect, she turned and walked away with my passport, leaving me standing at the window with my thoughts and a suitcase full of Chinese Bibles.

It seemed like two hours but was probably two minutes before she returned and barked something at the guard at the window as she handed my passport back to her. She gave me one more icy glare before turning and disappearing again. I didn't smile this time. The immigration guard stamped my passport and handed it back to me without any explanation. Once I had it back in my hand, I did smile at her, picked up my suitcase, and headed for customs.

I don't know what happened to the hundreds of people who were in the immigration area, but when I stepped into the customs room, there were about ten uniformed guards on one side of the room facing a short conveyer belt that was on the opposite side of the room. The conveyer belt had an X-ray machine in the middle of it. The only other person in there was an elderly Chinese woman who was struggling with a couple of large cardboard boxes that were tied up with string.

All luggage was expected to go through the X-ray machine. As I stepped into the room, I noticed all the guards' heads turn and look my way. I didn't make eye contact but said one of those quick prayers to get me through this. The conveyer belt was going right to left through the X-ray machine. This woman was trying her best to lift these boxes onto it. I decided to help her out. I walked over to the X-ray machine and set my suitcase down with my left hand on the floor about midway through the length of the X-ray machine. I then began to put this lady's boxes on the conveyer belt for her.

When they came out the other side of the X-ray machine, I helped her get them off the belt and onto her cart, never turning around to see if the guards were watching or not. Once she was loaded up, she said something, which I'm sure was a thank you of some kind, and I reached back over with my right hand and picked up my suitcase off the floor and helped escort this woman out the door. I never did look back at the guards, and my suitcase never touched the conveyer belt and was never X-rayed.

I wouldn't be surprised to find out someday that this elderly woman turned out to be an angel sent for that particular purpose to help me get a suitcase of Bibles into the hands of believers who desperately needed them. I met up with the rest of the team, and we traveled the trains, the subways, and on foot and actually found this large three-story building in a back alley being used as an underground church.

The pastor of this church has written several books on the persecuted church and is quite well-known internationally. He tried to encourage us to stay for the evening service they were going to have, but we had to get back out of the country before sundown. It was good to know that our small sacrifices were to be multiplied all over that particular part of the world. I'm sure those Bibles are still being used by someone today. We made it out without incident. I slept well that night.

> Do not fear, for those who are with us are more than those who are with them.
> —2 Kings 6:16

CHAPTER 22

PAPERS PLEASE

A chance came up to actually be able to visit South Sudan and help minister to our newly founded churches in this war-torn part of the world. Dave and I had already had success in Khartoum, Sudan, twice, but South Sudan would be an entirely different animal. We planned out the trip that would take place after leading a Work & Witness team in Ethiopia for a couple of weeks.

The plan was to complete that project and get those guys safely on the plane back to the USA, and we would stay behind in Ethiopia. There were no direct flights from Addis Ababa, Ethiopia, to Juba, South Sudan. We would have to fly through Nairobi, Kenya, first. Once we got there, we would catch a smaller plane from Nairobi to Juba. We figured if we were going to South Sudan, we might as well try to take a set of JESUS Film equipment with us. It would be a big benefit for evangelism to our brothers and sisters in the Juba area.

The problem was that we would first have to get the equipment into Ethiopia, then Kenya, and then Juba. There was no way to check it directly through. It's much easier to circumvent X-ray machines when you have a larger group of people traveling together with multiple carts of luggage. So getting into Ethiopia wasn't much of a problem.

After we completed our project in Ethiopia and dropped off the team to head home, Dave and I and three other church leaders caught our plane to Nairobi with our film equipment checked in. The airport in Nairobi has had a bad reputation of "losing" luggage over the years. We prayed that the Lord would protect His luggage from disappearing in the baggage handling area. The Lord did His part, and we were happy to see those bags of equipment come out, and we officially entered Kenya with no issues at all. Two down, and one to go.

We had to change airlines in Nairobi and brought all our stuff to the desk to check in. Still, there were no problems. As we walked out to the tarmac to load up, I noticed we were going to be flying on a small prop plane. The kind that seats twenty to thirty not so comfortably. I thought to myself, *Well, at least it's not a long flight.*

We had never been to Juba before. South Sudan claimed it as their capital. At this time, South Sudan was not even recognized as a sovereign nation by the world but considered it still part of Sudan. They had been fighting for their independence for twenty years and seemed close to getting it. A lot of the refugees who had fled the south into neighboring countries and to the north were now beginning to trickle back into the region. A sense of hope and a future was taking hold as new churches were being established. Visions of building a ministry center in Juba just might materialize. We were going to check it out, but first, we had to get in.

We made our approach for our landing. You could see the White Nile River flowing nearby, and the landscape was much greener than the area around Khartoum in the north. We exited the plane and walked toward the small terminal with the rest of the passengers. As we were walking, I was fumbling for my passport and praying that the JESUS Film equipment would get through the customs protocol that it's never been to before.

I had my passport in hand and continued to walk when I noticed everybody else who was on the flight had their passports out as well. But they also had about a six by nine–inch official-looking piece of card stock with their passport photo attached to it. I quickly looked at the other four guys who were with me, and they didn't have this document. They just had their passports like me.

We passed through the double doors and into the terminal and were immediately put into two lines for the immigration process. I looked off to the right and saw search tables set up in the customs area and plenty of South Sudanese military who ran the whole process. We stood in the back of the line as we slowly moved forward.

I watched as the other passengers handed their passports and this mystery document to the rather large immigration official. That's when I leaned over to Dave and asked, "Are we supposed to have something besides our passport to get into South Sudan?" That got him looking around and wondering.

As each passenger was admitted through immigration, they were instructed to pick up their luggage, which was lying right there, and put it on the search tables for the customs officials to hand search. I started thinking, *This is going to be interesting.* The five of us inched our way to the counter and handed over our passports to this military official. He asked for our other documents, which we obviously didn't have.

Apparently we were supposed to go to an office somewhere in Addis Ababa, Ethiopia, and apply for this official mystery document. None of us knew anything about it. We tried to explain our ignorance to the whole process, and all he said was, "Wait here." I thought this might be a really short trip. Even if they let us in with no papers, they were going to go through our luggage just a few steps away and grill us on what we were doing trying to get this electronic equipment into their country. My mind was playing out different scenarios of how this would end. None of it looked good.

We waited patiently for the official to come back from the phone call he was making. I turned to the right to see all that luggage of the other passengers being rifled through by the military on the search tables. The passengers helplessly stood there watching and occasionally picking up an item of theirs that would hit the floor from their bag. I saw our bags sitting there on the floor just a few feet away from all the activity.

Finally our man came back to the five of us and said, "You're supposed to have a travel permit to get into the country. I want you to go to the government office of South Sudan here in Juba and get your permit and then have it signed by the minister. When you come here to leave, I want to see it, or you will not leave. Is that understood?" All five of us shook our heads in unison and said, "Yes sir. Thank you, sir." He then handed us the address of the government office.

This whole process took a little bit of time, and our waiting ride outside was beginning to get impatient. As we turned away from the immigration desk to pick up our bags to head to the dreaded customs process, our driver came walking up and said, "Let's go!"

We said, "OK," and picked up all our bags, walked past everyone still getting searched, and went right out the doors and into a waiting vehicle. We had no papers and never got searched, and there we were in the country illegally. That was one scenario that didn't cross my mind when I was standing in line.

Come to find out, our driver who came in to get us was a church member but also was a captain in the South Sudanese military and was known by the other military in the airport. No one said a word to us. A seventh set of JESUS Film equipment had entered into the borders of Sudan.

In our brief stay in Juba, we couldn't travel too far because the roads were still mined and the rivers had bandit groups patrolling them. We were able to visit several small local villages and share our testimonies and encourage believers who were there. We were also able to visit the government office of Southern Sudan. We received our travel permit and then had a chance to visit the minister at his own house. He welcomed us with bottles of soda and biscuits as we sat with him on his patio. He happily signed and stamped our mystery documents.

> Trust in the Lord with all your heart, and lean not on your own understanding; In all your ways acknowledge Him, and He shall direct your paths.
> —Proverbs 3:5–6

CHAPTER 23

OF SNAKES AND SUCH

We were on one of our Amazon jungle excursions with Doc Garman. Our purpose was to build another wooden church structure, for another congregation, in another Aguaruna Indian village. After many hours in the boats, we pulled up to the river bank of this village. The guys unloaded all the supplies and gear we were to use and climbed up the steep bank to get to the village. The bank was so high, you wouldn't have known that there was even a village there unless you already knew it. I was glad I wasn't driving. We'd still be going down that river.

We were directed to the hut that we would call home for the next couple of nights. Typically these villages would construct one or two "gang beds" inside these huts for us. The beds would run the length of the hut on one or both sides and be off the dirt floor a foot or two and be made of bamboo. When we would show up, we would string our mosquito nets one by one the length of this crude platform. This setup caused us to sleep side by side with only the mosquito netting in between us. It's not the best way to get a restful night's sleep with a neighbor twenty inches on each side of you, but it was the safest.

Those nets provided protection from mosquitos and other creatures that may want to nibble on you or crawl into your bedding with you for a warm rest throughout the night. The only time you could get into trouble was if you rolled over and found yourself tight against the netting itself. That could leave you vulnerable to a nighttime bite by a hungry insect, bat, or some other being. And yes, that would happen from time to time.

I always tried to stay in the middle of my net. And I always brought my boots into the net with me for the night. You never knew if a spider or scorpion or worse would be passing by looking for a home for the evening. Finding one the wrong way would tend to ruin your morning.

It was later on in the day when we arrived, so we settled in and checked out the site where the church was to be built. It was located near the edge of the village. The villagers also showed us a watering hole where we could bathe at the end of the workday.

A lot of these villages will use the main river they are located on for bathing and washing, but the river was fairly strong and deep where this village was, and it would be very difficult to use it for these purposes. But as we walked out of the village and past the church site, there was a path that wound through the jungle for about an eighth of a mile before it went down to a grassy pond-like inlet that was somehow fed from the main river. There were some village women present and washing some pots and pans when we arrived to check it out. We thought, *This will work*. And we headed back up the trail to the village to settle in for the night.

As we got ready to crawl into our mosquito net cocoons for the night, one of the guys saw a rather large spider (actually very large) in the hut near his stuff. He proceeded to grab his boot to smack him…but missed. The spider disappeared in there somewhere, and we couldn't find him. So not only was he in the hut with us, but now he was not in the best of moods.

Things settled down as best they could, and we lay in our bunks in that dark hut, hoping the guys on either side of me wouldn't serenade me too much throughout the night with their snoring. Before I went to sleep, I started thinking about how blessed I was to be back in the jungle again to help out. Just a couple of weeks before, I had been in Venezuela in another part of the Amazon to help there with the Yanomamö tribe.

The night passed without incident—we never did find that spider—and the next morning, we rose to a full day of work. We worked late into the afternoon before we shut down. When we finished for the day, the guys went back to the hut to grab their towels and soap to head down to the watering hole for an evening bath. I stayed on the job site a little longer to lay some stuff out so it would be ready to go in the morning. When I finished, the guys had already passed me on the path to get their baths.

I went back to the hut to grab my towel and soap and tried to hustle to meet the guys down at the watering hole. As I walked past the church and down the path and got closer to the watering hole, I saw the guys were already done and drying off. Some of them passed by me on their way back to the village. By the time I stepped into the water, the rest of the team was done and gone, and I found myself alone at the watering hole.

I figured I'd be there a few minutes and then catch up with them for dinner. The water was about chest deep and had a fallen tree that lay in part of it that was perfect to put your soap and shampoo on as you stood next to it in the water. I waded out past my waist and noticed that the sun was going down and dusk had set in. I could begin hearing noises coming from the jungle that wouldn't normally bother me, but they weren't coming from the direction of the village. I was beginning to question my wisdom of being alone in the Amazon at dusk and not being at the apex of the food chain at feeding time.

Then my mind went back to that recent trip to the jungle in Venezuela and some of the fresh stories I heard in a few of those villages. In one village, a group of guys had gone hunting for food and separated in the jungle. They soon heard one of the guys screaming, and they all rushed to the location to find their comrade wrapped up by an anaconda. They quickly employed their machetes and freed their brother without harm to him but with much harm to the snake.

Then we went to another village where a man told us about how he was hunting alone in the jungle and was standing next to a large tree. Before he knew it, an anaconda had snuck up on him, latched onto his thigh, and tried to wrap him up. But because he was next to the tree, the snake was unable to wrap him and the tree, and this man was able to reach his machete and cut the head off this large and hungry reptile.

These memories were not comforting to me at this moment. I began to scrub a bit quicker, looking in all directions. I knew that when an anaconda attacks it usually will latch onto a thigh with its mouth and hang on as it wraps up its prey. I also knew I didn't have a machete. I was beginning to feel like I had a neon sign blinking over my head that said "Eat Here!"

I finished with the soap and quickly launched some shampoo onto my head, still looking around. That's when my mind said, *If I were an anaconda, this would be a perfect place to hang out. Chest high, grassy water, just off the main river, it would be easy pickings to…* Right at that moment, an unseen fish swam up to me and bit me on the thigh. I thought I was a dead man. The fish was probably about six inches long and just gave me a nibble, but in my state of mind it was a twenty-two-foot hungry anaconda.

Needless to say, I didn't stick around. I think I beat the guys back to the hut. Never again would I bathe alone in the jungle. I would always take someone slower than me. The Bible talks about Peter walking on the water, but I can testify that it's also possible to run on the water.

> Behold, I give you the authority to trample on serpents and scorpions, and over all the power of the enemy, and nothing shall by any means hurt you."
> —Luke 10:19

CHAPTER 24

THE ROAD TO DAMASCUS

I had caught wind of a need in Syria from one of our contacts in Jordan. There was a church under construction within Damascus that was being worked on by a lot of volunteers who were mostly refugees from neighboring countries. He asked if we were interested in helping out, and we said, "Yes." Now Syria is not a place where you want to take a big work team from the USA. That just wouldn't be a wise move. Besides, not many in the USA would want to sign up to go to Syria in the first place. But there were three of us who had extensive overseas and construction experience who signed up. We were soon on our way to Damascus.

Our Jordanian contact was to set up the field arrangements, and we were to meet him there. We knew to enter these Islamic countries that surround Israel that you had to have a passport that showed you had never been to Israel before, or they wouldn't let you into their country. The three of us had all been to Israel in the past, so we all had gotten new passports before we left so that Israeli stamp would not be in them.

We arrived in Vienna, Austria, and got ready for our last leg of our flights. After some vigorous questioning at the gate in Vienna by Syrian officials, we loaded onto the plane and took to the skies. The three of us reminded each other about protocol on foreign soil including the number 1 subject to never talk about in another country. And that would be politics. It just never ends well and can turn dangerous in certain situations to offer your well-meaning opinions. It's best to avoid it at all costs.

Our contact met us at the airport, and we were taken through the streets of Damascus to an apartment building where we would be staying with a Christian couple from a local church. The accommodations were more than adequate, and we were treated with true Middle Eastern hospitality by our hosts. Every meal was a feast as ladies from the church tried to outdo each other in bringing us their best dishes.

We settled in that first night and sat around getting to know our Syrian hosts a bit better. Then they started talking about what they thought about our government. Then they moved on to what they thought our government was up to in that region. I looked at the other guys and could see smoke starting to come out of their ears, but they did well in holding their tongues. It was soon after that that one of us said, "Well, we have a long day ahead of us tomorrow, I guess we should turn in." That ended that.

After another incredible meal the next morning, we were on our way to the job site. As we rode, I looked out the side window, and it seemed like everywhere I turned my head, there was a picture of their president. He was on billboards and posters and storefronts. It seemed like he was watching you wherever you went. Maybe that was the point.

The job site was an existing concrete building in the city that the church had purchased. They had gutted the structure and were in the process of putting it back together. We arrived to help with the concrete finishing and plastering stages of the reconstruction. We were introduced to the other workers on the site. They were all refugees who had fled Iraq. One of them was Kurdish, but all of us worked together as a team. It didn't take long to build authentic relationships with our new friends as love and humor crosses over a lot of cultural and language barriers.

Our days were spent getting dusty with each other, and in the evenings, we would clean up and go visiting in a section of town where the refugees were living. For the most part, we would listen as we shared tea, and these families would share their stories of the horrors they fled in Iraq.

One teenage boy told us in detail how he and his father were arrested together by government officials and then separated. They ended up killing his father but let him go. Now he was there in Syria trying to take care of his mother and his many siblings.

Apartment after apartment, the stories were similar. There wasn't much we could do but listen and pray with them. Just letting them talk seemed to be part of the healing process. Several days and nights passed as the routine became predictable. It was work during the day and visitations at night.

After a couple of days of building relationships on the job site, the Kurdish man began to share more with us. This guy had a great attitude and sense of humor. I guess he was becoming more comfortable with us. He shared his experience with us one day and why he left his home in Northern Iraq.

He told us how the Iraqi officials would come to his village and randomly pick someone out. Then they would strap an explosive vest on this individual and order him to start walking away from them and into a local field. At some point, with all the soldiers watching, the vest would be detonated. He said it was a game for them, and it would happen often.

This Kurdish man was not a Christian and had never been to a church to worship but thought it was right to help out on this project since the church was helping him put his life back together in Syria.

We knew there was a service coming up in a couple of nights and invited him to come. It was a long shot.

Our local hosts couldn't have treated us any better during our stay. But every evening, they would bring up that dreaded topic that we knew was forbidden, and we would constantly change the subject to avoid it. It was frustrating, especially with their president looking at you no matter where you went. I was proud of our guys for behaving in this area, even though each of us felt like giving a passionate rebuttal.

The night came for us to go to a church service at a different local church than the one we were working on. This church was located in the old walled city of Damascus. It was made up of a lot of different refugees from a variety of different countries. They were from Sudan, Iraq, and from all over the Middle East. There were former Muslims from Shiite and Sunni branches of Islam (they don't like each other very much) and many others. And of course, there would be many Syrians there as well. They had asked me to preach that night.

I told the other two guys that they may want to sit by a door in case something goes south. Who do you think that crowd would go after first? Of course, I was kidding…somewhat. As we pulled into the old city, we parked in a parking area on a main street that was called Straight Street and then began to walk down some ancient side streets or alleys. We turned a couple of corners and were almost there when we passed one section of a continuous building on the right that was called the House of Ananias. We went about fifty more yards, and our church was on the left.

The aged church was packed and even had people in the overflow in the outside courtyard. Standing behind the podium and looking out at that diverse crowd in this ancient and historic setting was quite a humbling experience. Even though my two comrades sat on the aisle, nothing went south that night. In fact, it went quite well. During the sermon, I looked out, and in the back corner of that crowd sat our Kurdish friend with a smile on his face. He had never been in a church service before.

I figured if the apostle Paul could get straightened out in this neighborhood, why couldn't anyone else? Our friend didn't accept the Lord that night, but he was there and heard the Gospel, and that was a huge step for him. The day is coming soon when we won't have to worry about governments or politics anymore but just enjoy each other's company as brothers and sisters. That day couldn't come soon enough.

> So the Lord said to him, "Arise and go to the street called Straight, and inquire at the house of Judas for one called Saul of Tarsus, for behold, he is praying. And in a vision he has seen a man named Ananias coming in and putting his hand on him, so that he might receive his sight."
> —Acts 9:11–12

CHAPTER 25

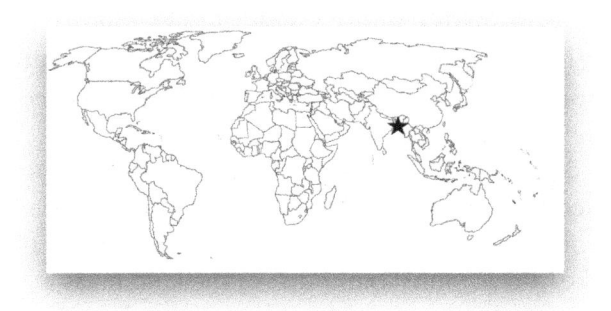

RICE AS FAR AS YOU CAN SEE

Bangladesh has a special place in my heart. It was the first place we landed when Dave and I were asked to try and establish the Work & Witness program in the South Asia field. Through the many trips there, eternal relationships have been established. We also helped out by taking different ministry materials like JESUS Film equipment into the country.

One of the other items taken in was something called the Proclaimer. It was the size of a tabletop radio and looked like one too. You could plug it in to power it, or you could crank it to charge it if no power was available. There was even a small solar panel on top if you wanted to go that route. These proclaimers were basically full audio Bibles where the Scriptures could be heard narrated in the local language depending on where you took them. I thought it was a clever tool to be used where electricity wasn't common and maybe the population had a low literacy rate.

Dave and I led numerous teams to Bangladesh and spent a lot of time traveling north and south to get to various project sites. Most of these trips were white-knuckle rides on the main roads leading in and out of the capital city of Dhaka. In this part of the world, everyone uses the highways. We would see overcrowded buses and trucks to cars and motorcycles to bicycles and men pulling loaded wagons by foot to herds of animals complete with their young shepherd guides. We were even delayed one time in the north as an elephant was being led down and across the highway by foot. You don't see that every day.

The things you do see every day, no matter where you travel there, are rice and people. Bangladesh is roughly the size of the state of Illinois with a population the size of half the USA crammed onto it. If you take into account that much of the land mass is rice paddies that are submerged in water, it doesn't leave much room for all those people.

The roads have been built up to stay out of the water, which is the reason every living organism uses them. As you travel these roads, you can't help but notice just how large many of these rice fields are. Some looked like they went on forever…as far as the eye could see.

I learned that several large companies owned much of this land and would hire the people in the small villages to work the fields. These humble villages were numerous and sprinkled throughout the country.

With limited options available to these villagers, most would stay and work the local fields around their villages. Pay was low, and no education was available for the children there. One of our main purposes in going to South Asia was to give the children an opportunity for education.

Through the efforts of Dave and his brother Glen in establishing the foundation named Compassion575, funds were raised to establish and support a number of Child Development Centers, or CDCs as we call them. These CDCs would average in size from thirty to seventy children in attendance and offer them an education, a meal (sometimes the only good meal for the day), and basic meds that weren't normally available or affordable where they lived.

All this was great, but they also needed a place to meet. That's where the work teams came in. We would go and build the structures in these predominantly Hindu and Muslim villages. You could say we raised a few eyebrows when we showed up to mix mortar and lay bricks all day in that tropical heat.

One place was so hot that I was concerned about the team's stamina. It wasn't quite as hot as the Torch in chapter 14, but it was close. The locals could not fathom that a group of Westerners would be working in these conditions. Many times we would be asked in different villages, "Why are you doing this? Why are you here?"

This would open a door for us to tell them, "Jesus has changed our hearts, and because of that, we love you and your children, and that's why we do this." They couldn't comprehend this concept. The only Westerners they had ever seen or heard about would stay in fancy hotels or just pass through in an air-conditioned vehicle. Nobody ever lived with them or worked for them in this way. They had a government that didn't pay attention to these "fringe" people, but they were experiencing that there is a God Who did. They were blown away.

On one of these projects close to the southern coast of the Bay of Bengal, there was a village that backed up to a large natural forest. A small river separated them from each other. We learned that at night, a large Bengal tiger would come across the river from the forest and pick out what he wanted to eat for the evening. Almost daily, we would hear of a dog or cow that had been on the previous night's menu. There was even a man who worked with us who had survived a tiger attack in the past…and he had the scars to prove it! I was conversing with a group of half a dozen local men who had been discussing the history of this tiger. When I suggested they should tie a bell around his neck, they all looked at me sideways. Eventually they laughed, and I went back to work.

Amazing things grew out of these simple brick structures. The CDCs were a success during the week, and on the weekends, the buildings would be used as churches. Soon self-help groups for women were popping up. They were a type of local microeconomic program. The local wives of the community would meet and pool resources together and borrow from it as needed to start up a small business and then pay it back through their profits. They would be simple businesses like baking bread and selling it. But it gave the women a sense of purpose in a society where they had none. Dave and I had the privilege to sit in on a few of these meetings in different areas.

Another purpose for these brick structures was protection from the frequent storms. The CDC building was almost always the only brick building in the village. Bangladesh is frequently hit by strong storms and/or flooding. Now the people had a place to go for protection. One European company heard of what was being done there and invested in their own projects of building even larger and stronger concrete structures for the people and that was fine with us.

On one of the project sites in a remote section of the northern part of the country, we were working on the edge of a huge rice crop (surprise, surprise). As we worked through the heat of the morning, I kept hearing something coming from the direction of the village. It was distant, and I wasn't always able to hear it with all the noise on the job site, but every once in a while, I could. It sounded like a radio playing, which I found highly unusual in a remote village like this with no electricity.

Soon it was lunchtime, and we laid our tools down and headed toward the village for some shade and food. The local ladies had been preparing lunch for us this day. As we got closer to the village, I heard that radio again. When we got to where we would get our plate of local rice, I saw it sitting on the window opening of this hut where the group of ladies had been working all morning.

To my surprise, it wasn't a radio at all, it was a Proclaimer. These ladies had been listening to the Bible all morning as they worked. It was the first time I had ever seen or heard one in action like that. I'm sure we had brought it into the country on one of our previous trips. Sometimes God lets you see a seed you planted for Him as it is growing into fruit.

When we would finish the construction on each of these CDCs, we would always have a dedication service to open them. These would be full-blown church services thanking and praising Jesus Christ for what He's done and going to do in and through that particular building. It always amazed me to see how many people would show up for these dedication services.

Almost the entire crowd would be Hindu or Muslim, and at some there would be over a thousand in attendance. They didn't mind sitting there listening to us praising God and telling them about Jesus Christ. Usually the Hindu leader of the community and the Muslim leader would stand up and address the crowd. They would publicly thank us for coming and, more importantly, for loving their children in a place that could care less about them. It always stunned me when they would do that. In a land that is full of rice and people, the majority of efforts in the past have always been to harvest the rice. We are now seeing that God is harvesting the souls of the people.

> Then He said to His disciples, "The harvest truly is plentiful, but the laborers are few. Therefore pray the Lord of the harvest to send out laborers in His harvest."
> —Matthew 9:37–38

CHAPTER 26

STEPHEN

I introduced you to Stephen back in chapter 13 and mentioned him again in chapter 14. He's the one who told me that only the ancients make cope with cow urine as we headed to "the Uttermost." He was also there in Gambella, the Torch, when we had issues with the JESUS Film equipment two nights in a row.

When I first met Stephen, he was probably in his mid to late twenties. He had a small frame and stood about 5'10". He was from the Sudanese tribe called the Nuer. This also meant that he was very dark. Another distinctive feature of the males from the Nuer tribe is their physical markings across their foreheads. Many of the Sudanese tribes have unique markings or scarring to tell which tribe you are from.

We never got a straight answer as to why these tribes do this. One theory is that the English started it to tell the tribes apart during the slave trading days. Another theory is that the tribes marked themselves in an attempt to make the English not want them. I don't know for sure how it started, but the tribes wear these markings as a badge of honor today.

The Nuer villages will have a guy who will take care of this as the boys of the village reach the so-called age of manhood. He will proceed to cut horizontal lines across the young man's forehead that stretch from the top of one ear to the other. He may make half a dozen cuts in this way. As the wounds heal, they leave the distinctive scarring that identifies you as a Nuer. There is no mistaking it.

Stephen had these markings and a few times asked me if I wanted to go see "the guy" to have mine done. I always told him I'd think about it and then would change the subject. Stephen had a gentle spirit about him, and I never really saw him get rattled. Even when things didn't work out like they were supposed to, he just went with the flow.

In the Wild West atmosphere that is the extreme western part of Ethiopia and the borderlands of Eastern Sudan, Stephen was in charge of the JESUS Film Ministry. He didn't care who he was showing this film to; he just wanted to share this Gospel story with as many people as possible…and he did. I understood that he was credited as the first man personally responsible for showing the JESUS Film to over one million people. And he did this while he was so young.

As I have mentioned before, many tribes do not like each other. In fact, some of these tribes have been warring with each other for generations. That didn't seem to matter to Stephen. The love that he had from God for his fellow man superseded any of that nonsense.

I'd watch Stephen when we would show the JESUS Film to the Anuak tribe. They were notorious for not getting along with the Nuer. Stephen would wear a knit cap and pull it down over his forehead to his eyebrows so you couldn't see his tribal markings. He also stayed in the shadows to be discrete about his presence there. He didn't want anything to take away from the message that was being presented on the screen. Friend or foe, it didn't matter; Stephen just wanted them all to know about Jesus.

You can imagine my surprise when I got word one day that Stephen had passed away. Apparently he suddenly contracted some type of stomach issue and was dead within days. Talk about a shocker. The age-old questions came up: "Why would God take someone so young? Couldn't God have protected a servant like Stephen from this type of fate? Of all the people on the earth spreading the Gospel, why would God take one who was doing so much?"

We all know someone who has been taken too soon in our eyes. I've known quite a few. We'll never have answers as to why this happens except to trust that God knows what He's doing. We live in a broken world that we broke ourselves, and part of that brokenness is that we all live under a created dynamic called time.

We weren't designed to live within time at the start of creation. We were as free as free could be. But since the fall of man, we've been shackled into a mindset of having limited time on earth. We do everything we can to beat it, conserve it, and try not to waste it. We forget that we all live forever because we can't grasp that ultimate reality due to the so-called time reality we're caught in for now.

God has promised us eternity from conception; it just depends on where we want to spend it. I try to think outside the "time" box whenever I hear that we've lost another friend way too soon. What is seventy to ninety years of physical time in the realm of eternity anyway? Does it still hurt to lose friends and loved ones? Absolutely, and it always will. But we must remember that our physical days here are just a vapor, no matter how long we live.

The apostle Paul told us that Jesus has taken the sting out of death for those who've put their trust in Him. I don't know who this chapter is for, but I encourage you to do your best to think outside the "time" box when dealing with another shocking announcement.

Stephen did what he was supposed to do in his limited time here on earth. He had eternal impacts on hundreds of thousands of people. I just felt that his story needed to be heard now—in this time. Because I'm pretty sure you'll hear it again when we're no longer bound by created time. It's up to us to pick up the mantle of those like Stephen and carry on.

> For I am already being poured out as a drink offering, and the time of my departure is at hand. I have fought the good fight, I have finished the race, I have kept the faith. Finally, there is laid up for me the crown of righteousness, which the Lord, the righteous Judge, will give to me on that Day, and not to me only but also to all who have loved His appearing.
> —2 Timothy 4:6–8

CHAPTER 27

ONE VOICE IN THE NIGHT

We were with Doc on one of our many adventures to the Amazon. It had been a good trip up to this point as we were in the midst of building several churches for the Aguaruna tribe. The Work & Witness team of guys was settled into one of the jungle villages. There was still another day's worth of work to do to complete this particular project.

The guys had been invited one evening to travel to a nearby Aguaruna village and show the JESUS Film with a JESUS Film team who was in the area. Some of the guys decided to stay in the village where the project was because of the logistics involved in this venture, and some of us took full advantage of the opportunity before us. I never wanted to miss a chance to witness God at work.

When we arrived, it looked very similar to all the rest of the Aguaruna villages I had been in. It had the beautiful simplistic layout of the stick huts with thatch roofs. They were sprinkled up and down winding dirt paths against a backdrop of the thick Amazon forest.

These villages always seemed to be located right on or just off the local main waterway, and this village was no exception.

We arrived by boat, climbed up the steep embankment off the river, and headed down the well-worn path. We passed by several huts as we came to a large clearing. There were some huts lining the outside of this clearing, and from what I could tell, this must have been the village square, or "downtown." The clearing was large enough to easily accommodate the couple hundred local inhabitants. This was where the JESUS Film would be shown this night.

As the sun began to set, we started to help the film team set up the screen and sound system to get ready for the showing. We knew that once the sun went down, we were going to be staying in this village until the next morning. It was just too dangerous to be on those rivers at night. So one of these huts would be our bunkhouse until sun up.

As we waited, a meal of eggs was prepared for us for dinner, which was quite nice considering what it could have been. I noticed a chicken that was tied up just outside of a hut that we soon discovered was to be our house for the night. I figured she was the source of the eggs, so I went over and thanked her after the meal in my elementary Spanish. We then went to get the film started.

When we got to the clearing a crowd had already gathered. There were about 150–200 there. I had seen larger crowds gather for a JESUS Film showing, but there was something about this gathering. It felt more intimate as the villagers clustered together on the ground in front of the screen. The stars had come out, which just added to the setting. You will have a hard time on earth finding a more beautiful sky than a deep clear cloudless star-filled sky in the Amazon jungle.

As the JESUS Film started, I noticed it was in the Spanish language, which I found a bit strange since a lot of Aguaruna don't speak much Spanish. As I was sorting all that out in my head, I saw a man stand up in the midst of the huddled mass of sitting people and begin talking loudly. I wasn't quite sure what to make of this scene.

I knew he wasn't speaking Spanish, but he kept on talking as the film played on. It didn't seem to bother anyone else. In fact, they acted like he wasn't even there as they continued to stare at this lit-up screen with the fascinating moving pictures of people on it.

It finally dawned on me that this man was speaking Aguaruna. The JESUS Film had not been translated into the Aguaruna language at this time. This man was translating the film, word for word, from Spanish to Aguaruna. And he was doing it loud enough for everyone around him to hear and understand. I watched in awe for the next two hours as this man never sat down, wavered, or hesitated. He only got a break when the reels were changed three times.

For two hours, he told the whole Gospel of Luke—from the angel visiting Mary to the empty tomb. When the film had ended, I wondered how well he had done in capturing the Spirit through the language barrier. But when I saw a few dozen Aguaruna come forward to accept Christ after a simple invitation, I knew it was the Lord Who had spoken through him the past two hours.

As I lay in the darkness on my bamboo bed that night, I was pondering what I had just witnessed. In all the JESUS Film showings I have been a part of, I had never seen anything like that before. The size of the crowd didn't matter. What mattered was that they were *all* made in the image of God Himself. That means He loved them enough to make sure they had a chance to hear about Jesus in their own language through a man obedient and sacrificial enough to stand there for two hours and translate the Gospel loud enough for all of them to hear it. How cool was that? It truly was a beautiful night.

We woke up early the next morning to head back to the village where we had been working. A nice chicken breakfast was prepared for us before we headed down to the river. I thought this was quite nice. As I took my second bite, I realized the chicken I had thanked for the eggs the night before was no longer tied up at the spot where she had been. In fact, I didn't see her anywhere. So if you ever ask me that age-old question of what comes first…I guess I would have to answer, the egg.

> He is the image of the invisible God, the firstborn over all creation. For by Him all things were created that are in heaven and that are on earth, visible and invisible, whether thrones or dominions or principalities or powers. All things were created through Him and for Him.
> —Colossians 1:15–16

CHAPTER 28

(   )

It had become somewhat routine for us to take JESUS Film equipment into various countries. On several occasions, this was done when we were going into a country with a Work & Witness team for a building project. Dave and I went to some countries numerous times and watched the Lord blind eyes or whisper into guards' ears to turn and walk away as we approached their checkpoint. I called it somewhat routine, but we never took it for granted. We knew the Lord wanted this equipment to go into the very dark places of the world.

It wasn't always a full set of film equipment to be used for a large public audience that we took in. Technology was changing, and the ways to reach those caught in parts of the world where it was illegal or too dangerous to show the film publicly were changing as well.

Personal DVD players with encrypted DVDs and iPods downloaded with the JESUS Film and other evangelistic material were being produced for one-on-one evangelism. Today, multiple languages of the JESUS Film can be put on tiny SD cards. We took many of these tools with us to give to our contacts who would get them into the right hands within the underground church.

Many times we get accustomed to the freedom we have in the West when it deals with religion. Despite the feeling we are losing more of that freedom in today's climate, there are those in the world who have always lived under an oppressive cloud and constant threat of persecution for their faith.

We attended a quick baptism service in one country that was held inside with no cameras, no celebration, and in almost complete silence. If it were known that these ten individuals were making a public profession of faith for Jesus Christ by being baptized, they would be marked for execution. Their extended families would also pay the same price even though they had nothing to do with it. And yet these ten did it anyway.

One friend of ours shared his testimony with us. He grew up in a faith where the priests had all of the power in the community. They forbid anyone from owning a Bible. In fact, they taught people that if they ever touched a Bible, they would be struck dead instantly by God because they were too unworthy to handle God's Word. You can only imagine the power abuse this could lead to...and did.

As our friend grew up in this climate, he became more cynical and depressed with life and with what he saw as no hope. He looked for a way to end his life. Then he remembered the priest's orders that "if you ever touched a Bible, God would kill you." He went looking for a Bible to end his life. When he finally found one and picked it up, the lightning bolt never came. So he opened it up and began reading it. The Lord used His written Word to preach to this lost soul. Our friend found faith in a Savior named Jesus Christ Who gave him a new lease on life and a hope for the future. Our friend was now heading up the JESUS Film ministry in certain parts of his country.

Another testimony we listened to came from a former priest of a different faith. He wanted to have dinner but didn't want to be seen publicly with us in his community. He reserved a private room in the back of a local restaurant. When Dave and I arrived, he was already there. He shared with us over dinner how he came to faith in Christ.

He had traded tradition and religion in for a personal relationship with God. We were told that dozens of these priests were coming to the Lord but staying in their positions secretly for now. This way they could reach even more priests and congregations with the Gospel.

But it's not just those who are new to other faiths who face this type of fear. A Christian brother in one country had been dragged off from his home, thrown in the back of a pickup, and then beaten so badly that his captors thought he was dead. They took his body and threw him into a ditch by the side of the road. All this was done to him just because he professed to be a Christian. He eventually woke up and found his way back home to recover. A few months later, here he was interpreting for me as I was preaching in his area. He was still limping from his injuries.

There were some communities where we worked who wouldn't even allow the Christians to bury their dead locally just because they were Christians. Others weren't allowed to work because of their faith in Christ. The Christian community was treated as subhuman.

A few of us had an opportunity to worship with an underground church in a very dark corner of one country. The service was at night, and we were brought in by vehicle and ushered quickly into what seemed to be a house converted into a worship area. The small building was made of corrugated tin walls and roof. As the service started, everything was done in rather hushed tones.

I got up with the interpreter to share the message for the night. As we got into the message a bit, a huge bang interrupted my train of thought. Then another bang followed. Soon it became a constant banging. What I first thought was gunfire turned out to be a volley of rocks hitting the tin walls from outside. It was so loud, we couldn't continue and had to stop for a few minutes.

I did wonder about the safety of everyone in that room. By the look on the faces of the people there, it wasn't the first time this had happened to them. You can imagine how they must be treated publicly for their faith. Eventually the loud banging stopped. I guess their arms got tired. I halfway expected the peppering with the rocks to start up again at any moment. The thought also crossed my mind that they might return with something more powerful than rocks. We were able to finish the service without further interruptions. Only when our vehicle pulled up were we allowed to step outside and then be whisked away.

How can you not want to help brothers and sisters like this who face so much opposition for their faith in their everyday life? Different strategies were being implemented to encourage Christians living in these areas and to reach more with the Gospel. In one country, we built an underground Christian radio station that was totally encased within another building so it wouldn't be seen at all. The signal from this station would be sent to a different country that was not hostile to the Gospel. From that country, the signal would be piped into a third country where the Gospel was illegal. This way, the Christian broadcasting was entering that country in their own language from an undetected source. Nothing could be done to stop it.

There were also businesses we saw in operation that were basically fronts for underground Christian ministries. The Christian workers in these businesses would listen to conversations of patrons to see if anyone might be sensitive to the Gospel. They would then look for opportunities to share Jesus with them in a one-on-one situation. It was a methodical approach but was getting positive results.

There seems to be no end to these types of stories. This is why we would try to get as many tools as possible into the hands of our brothers and sisters who risk it all for their faith. The JESUS Film isn't just reaching hundreds or thousands at a time. Many times it is exposing the Gospel to one desperate soul at a time. This is happening through the efforts of our fellow believers who are sold out enough in their faith to risk everything just to give that opportunity of eternal life in Jesus Christ to others.

> The Holy Spirit testifies in every city, saying that chains and tribulations await me. But none of these things move me; nor do I count my life

dear to myself, so that I may finish my race with joy, and the ministry which I received from the Lord Jesus, to testify to the Gospel of the grace of God.

—Acts 20:23B–24

CHAPTER 29

MOROCCAN NIGHTS

Over the years and through many trips, a lot of contacts and relationships are established. I was asked to go on a trip by some close friends whom I had been with overseas many times. They had a contact who had been doing work in Morocco, and he was trying to get a small group of guys with carpentry experience together to work at an orphanage just outside of a major city in Morocco.

Of course, I wanted to help out any way I could and said, "Yes." The six of us were soon on the ground and traveling to a Christian Center close to the orphanage. This center would be our base during most of our stay there. We would get up in the mornings and head over to the orphanage to work for the day. Most of the projects were of the small woodworking variety, like building bookshelves, tables, and solving much-needed storage problems. But it was enough to fill our days.

The ladies who worked at this facility were more than appreciative and really took care of us at lunch times. But the stars of the show were the kids who lived there. They were all over us. In a society that saw them as throw-away kids, they were anything but. One little boy who was about six or seven had been born without arms. He was a bundle of energy and always with us as we worked. In fact, we had to keep an eye on him for his own safety. I never saw him without a smile on his face. It was an absolute blessing for us to be around them.

After several days of working, we had a day off and decided to go on a hike in the mountains behind the Christian Center where we were staying. The six of us went and took several of the women who worked at the center with us to get some exercise and enjoy God's creation.

As we started up the mountains, we came across a village after about twenty to thirty minutes of walking. We were told we needed to walk around the village and not go into it. It was a Muslim village, and they didn't like that a Christian Center was nearby. They would force anyone from that center to go around them. Sometimes they even threw rocks at them if they saw them. It seems like everybody around the world likes to throw rocks. We gladly went around. I wasn't in the mood to be peppered with rocks today.

We spent several hours walking up this mountain and came to a spot where we stopped and had a makeshift picnic. The scenery was fantastic. After a quick bite, the guys wanted to continue on up the mountain, but the ladies decided they had enough and wanted to return to the center. In that culture, women always need a male chaperone, so one of the guys accompanied them back down the trail.

As they approached that village, they noticed a lot of commotion happening within it. There was a lot of wailing and crying going on. There was so much of it that it piqued the interest and concern of our teammate who was with the ladies. He asked them if it would be OK to go check it out. They agreed, and he headed into the village alone. He came to one building in the center of the village where all of the noise was coming from. He said it looked like the whole village was gathered around and inside this building.

He made his way inside to see what the commotion was all about. Laying on the floor on a blanket was a frail man of about seventy with a woman holding his head in her lap as she sat on her knees. He was in agonizing pain. Our friend was told that this man had fallen into the village well, and they had just pulled him out. As our friend got closer to the man, he noticed a dirty rag laying across the man's leg. It seemed to be the major source of this man's discomfort. Our buddy was granted permission to take a look at the wound and was greeted with about four inches of broken leg bone sticking out through the skin. It was a serious compound fracture.

Even though this was a Muslim village, our friend asked if he could pray for the man. The people said yes, and he did. There wasn't much else he could do after that. There were no vehicles in this village. He didn't have the keys to our vehicle at the center. And the rest of us were going to be up in the mountains for a few more hours. So he left the village and went back down to the center with the ladies.

We returned about sundown and looked forward to some rest after a beautiful day. Then we were confronted with the story from the village. Right around that time, someone from the village showed up at the center asking for us to help. It was a big step for them to do this. We got our vehicle and headed back up to the village.

Once we arrived, we got out of the vehicle and walked into the center of the dark village. They led us to the house where this injured man had been laid. He looked terrible in that candlelit room, and it was apparent that his life was in jeopardy. Tucked away in the corner of the room was an old random door. We grabbed it and laid it next to the man. As gently as we could, we lifted him up and laid him on the door. We then picked up the door and carried him outside into the night. After navigating a few narrow pathways, we carefully slid him into the back of our vehicle's rear opening, door and all.

There was only room for two others in the vehicle after he was in there, so two of our team climbed in and slowly drove this man off the mountain and to the closest hospital in the nearest big city. We walked back to the center. When our teammates returned late that night, they said got him there in time and said, "We'll see what happens."

What we didn't expect to happen was the next day, we were visited at the center by someone from the village who informed us that the six of us were invited to dinner in the village. We accepted and made our way back up the mountain that evening. We were led into one of the homes there. We took our shoes off at the door and entered the main room of the house. We were instructed to sit on the floor in a circle. We obliged and were joined by the patriarch of the house who was somehow related to the man who fell in the well.

He didn't speak any English, but his message was coming across loud and clear. He was thankful that someone cared enough to help. His wife and daughters began the parade of bringing out trays full of food and setting them in the midst of the seven of us. Our host poured out some hot sweet mint tea to get things started. Then a big platter of chicken and rice came out. These settings always made me a little nervous because I'm left-handed. To use your left hand to eat in a Muslim culture is always a big no-no. I learned to just sit on it so I wouldn't be tempted to reach into the communal dish and cause an international incident. We followed all the proper protocols, and it was an incredible meal together.

It dawned on me later that it was September 11, 2006—the fifth anniversary of 9/11—and here we were having dinner with a Muslim tribe in their own village and house. God couldn't have made it more beautiful.

We soon left Morocco to come back to the States. We later learned that the man who fell into the well made a full recovery. We also heard that many people in that village accepted the Lord, and they no longer throw rocks at the ladies from the center but welcome them into the village every time they see them. The news of this whole event spread to all the other villages tucked away in those mountains. It always amazes me how we can plan out our schedules for the Lord and can accomplish them, but at the same time, He can use us to accomplish other plans that He has scheduled that we never saw coming.

> The people who sat in darkness have seen a great light, and upon those who sat in the region and shadow of death Light has dawned.
> —Matthew 4:16

CHAPTER 30

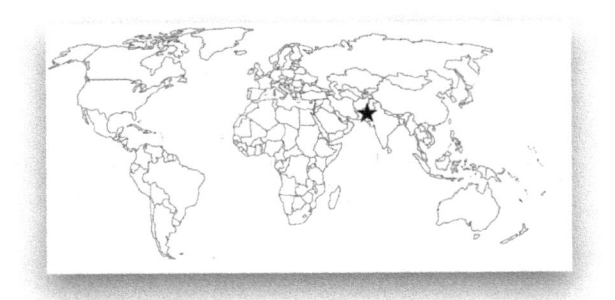

WHERE DID DAVE GO?

When Dave and I were asked to establish a Work & Witness program on the South Asia field for the Nazarene Church, this included several countries. The South Asia field is basically made up of the rim countries that surround India. India had become its own field. There were places like Nepal, Bangladesh, Sri Lanka, Pakistan, as well as some other countries that the church was trying to get a foothold in.

Obviously it would not be wise to take a group of volunteer Americans into some of these places, as you can imagine. But there was still a great need in all of these countries to reach them with the Gospel. Child Development Centers had been established to help with the educational and nutritional needs of the children in this region. Dave and his brother Glen had a big part in this endeavor through their Compassion575 efforts. I mentioned some of this back in chapter 25. We had found these CDCs to be a very fruitful ministry.

Pakistan had several of these CDCs established. They also had several JESUS Film teams who were in need of JESUS Film equipment. There are a few places in the world where the official church tends to not endorse sending its members. This is understandable due to the history of kidnapping and violence toward its missionaries that the church has had to deal with over the years. I totally get that concept. If they knew you had any plans on going to these areas, they would drop you a note of some kind just to make sure you knew that if you went, you were on your own. No negotiations would be made on your behalf if something sinister would befall you. That should be understood. If you negotiated for a release of a captive in one country, it would set off a firestorm of abductions all over the world by those looking to make a quick buck.

So thinking of going to Pakistan would warrant one of these clarifications. It wasn't the first time I had received one of these warnings. In fact, I had gotten them from our own State Department before. But Angie and I had always prayed for God's will, to go wherever it was, and we always received peace about the upcoming trip.

The way we looked at it was that I could be in a car accident right here in Virginia tomorrow going about normal life. Or I could be taken out trying to help thousands hear about a Savior Who came to offer them eternal life. Which way would you want to be taken out? If you're doing what God wants you to do, you are untouchable until He wants you home with Him. That is a key principle the Lord has taught Angie and me over the years. Besides, there are still so many who need an opportunity to make the right decision about their own eternity.

Our contact in Pakistan asked if we were interested and willing to go. Dave and I said, "Yes," and the arrangements were beginning to be put in place. Once we got there, we were to visit some of the CDCs to see how they were doing. We would also visit some churches and try to be an encouragement to our brothers and sisters there who have to endure so much for their faith. They didn't get many visitors from the West. Oh yeah...before we would do all this, we had to get a couple of sets of JESUS Film equipment into the country undetected.

A few weeks before our trip, I was praying and thinking about it. For some reason, the Lord impressed upon me to make some stickers. He showed me a credit card–sized sticker that had a flag on it and the words "Pakistan Child Development Center." I had learned to listen when the Lord would drop an idea into my spirit, so I quickly came up with a design. The sticker would have the green and white flag of Pakistan on the left and the words "Pakistan Child Development Center" printed next to it on the right.

I knew that in many of the foreign countries we would visit, a certain percentage of the security guards were illiterate. Of course, they were always holding the guns, but they typically may not have been exposed to educational opportunities that others had. So if you looked official or had official-looking documents or items with their national flag, they might let you pass. I was beginning to see what the Lord was up to.

With the help of a friend, because I was illiterate in how to create them, I was able to print up several sheets of these stickers. I kept them in my carry-on as Dave and I began our long trek to the other side of the world. We eventually landed in a large city in Pakistan and made it through the immigration process. This was another airport that neither one of us had been to before.

As we waited for our luggage to come out onto the belt, we both were checking out what we might expect for the next stage in customs. Finally our bags popped out on the belt, and we pulled them off to the side. I reached into my carry-on and found the sheets of stickers I had brought and handed a few sheets to Dave. We unlocked and unzipped our big luggage that had all the JESUS Film equipment in them and began plastering these small stickers all over any of the items and smaller bags that were inside. I had wanted to wait until now to do this so no red flags would be raised by our own TSA back home. They might not be too understanding if they saw large amounts of equipment with a bunch of Pakistani flags all over them.

Once Dave and I sufficiently covered everything in the bags, we zipped them back up and relocked them and loaded them onto a couple of carts. Dave had one complete set of equipment and I had another. Security was run by the Pakistan military. Dave went through in front of me with no problem at all and got to the other side of customs and kept walking, pushing his cart in front of him. I watched him disappear around a large column. He never looked back.

When my turn came up the uniformed guard looked at my luggage and then at me and motioned for me to go over to the search table. I humbly agreed and accompanied by two uniformed security detail I pushed all of my luggage over to a table that was against the wall. Dave was out of sight, and I could only picture him outside of the airport wondering what happened to me. I had a bit more pressing business to take care of first. I said a quick prayer for the Lord to help me out. My prayer would have been longer, but the search table was only about twenty feet away.

Once there, one of the gentlemen asked me to put my bags on the table. His English was good enough, and he looked like he outranked the other guy. I put my big bags up on the table. He then asked me, "What's in them?"

I calmly told him, "It is educational equipment for the children of Pakistan." He gave me one of those looks as if he was trying to read my face for any kind of clue that would contradict what I just told him.

Finally he said, "Open them."

In the back of my mind, I was picturing Dave at the hotel and here I am. I unzipped the first bag, and he asked me again, "What are all these bags?"

I told him again, "Its educational equipment for your children here in Pakistan." As he and his assistant began rifling through that large bag and started pulling out the smaller bags inside, all you could see was that every bag inside was adorned with a sticker that had a flag of Pakistan and the words "Pakistan Child Development Center" on them. The second guy pointed at one of the stickers and said something I couldn't understand to the first guy. Then something was said back to him as I stood there. I thought, *Dave is probably eating by now.*

The first soldier fired up the questioning again about my second bag. I gave the same response. "It's educational equipment for your children here in Pakistan." He asked me to open it as well. This time, they just looked into it and were greeted by more stickers that had their home flag on them. The second soldier pointed at it again, and they had a short conversation before they turned to me and told me to collect my things and go. I shook my head in affirmation and said, "Yes, sir."

They watched me as I reloaded my cart and walk away. I was silent on the outside as I walked away from them, but on the inside, I was having a conversation with the Lord. "You have done it again and did it the way You wanted to again. Using stickers of all things. Thank You, Lord!" As I got farther away from the welcoming committee, I came up on that big column where I saw Dave turn the corner and disappear. I got to the other side, and there was Dave still there with his cart.

He saw what had happened and was behind that column praying the whole time I was at the search table. We went through the doors together and into the night with equipment that would be used to reach thousands for Jesus Christ in a very dark corner of the world.

> This is the Lord's doing; it is marvelous in our eyes.
>
> —Psalm 118:23

CHAPTER 31

PASS THE YUCA PLEASE

We headed back to Peru to work with Doc again. There were only five of us going this time. We did our traditional travel of flying to Lima, then flying to Chiclayo, then driving over the Andes to the edge of the jungle. But instead of taking the road into the jungle that headed to the mission station that we had taken so many times before, we headed north for several hours before coming to another jungle border town. From there, we loaded into the back of a pickup and drove the winding dirt pathways that hugged the Andean foothills and deeper into a part of the Amazon jungle we had never seen.

After several more hours, we ran out of drivable path and arrived at some sort of an outpost. We unloaded our gear from the pickup as Doc went over to someone in charge to finalize some details. There were a couple of donkeys being loaded up with corrugated roofing and boxes of nails. We weren't going to be taking our normal mode of travel by boat on this trip. We were going to hike into the Amazon.

It's the only time I can recall that we used pack mules on a trip. As bad as I felt for them, I was glad we didn't have to carry all those supplies. It was bad enough having to carry my own backpack. Off we went into the unknown. There were four Aguaruna villages in this part of the jungle that all needed physical church structures. Our goal was to hike to them one by one, get as much done as we could, and then hike back out. It seemed like a pretty high bar to set since the most we've ever done in one trip were three churches.

We hiked over a pretty modern bridge as we left the outpost, but that would be the end of the modern world for the next week and a half. The trail soon turned into a pathway as the hours clicked off and we got deeper into the jungle. Since we were still in the foothills of the Andes, our path went up and down as well as winding back and forth. Sometimes we were next to a stream for a while, and other times I felt like we were climbing a mountain. We finally arrived at the first village.

We saw the fresh pile of lumber waiting for us. It had been recently cut from the surrounding forest by the villagers. We found our hut, settled in, and started prepping the building site with what sun we had left. Soon it would be dinnertime. You never quite knew what to expect when the local village was in charge of the meals. The main course could be just about anything. If you're lucky, you'd get a fish. And I mean the whole fish from head to tail. But there was one staple you could count on for every meal. There would always be a big platter of boiled yuca.

Yuca is a white starch root that is plentiful in the Amazon, and the Indians don't mind consuming mass quantities of it or sharing mass quantities of it. When boiled and served, they vary in size from a small potato to coffee mug size. The best way I can describe this tasteless root is that it's like eating a candle without the wick. But of course, I shared with you way back in chapter 2 the lesson to always eat what's put before you. So I would do my best to choke these suckers down.

We sat for dinner at a table prepped with banana leaves as place mats. Our plates came out to each of us containing a whole fish and a couple pieces of yuca. Then an extra platter of yuca was plopped on the table for everyone to belly up for seconds when we emptied our plates. We went to bed that night a bit tired from the hike but glad we had arrived without incident.

We worked hard the next morning, taking a few minutes off when we were called for breakfast. You guessed it...another big helping of yuca. We were soon back to work and really rolled on this first church to get it up. Of course, we were still rather fresh at this point in the trip.

Once we knocked it out, we loaded up our backpacks and mules and headed deeper into the jungle to the next village. We encountered more hills and more twists and turns.

Every once in a while, we would come to a ravine. You could either walk way around it, or to save time, there would be a manual "cable car" that was suspended across from both peaks. These cable cars were basically an open wooden box about three feet by five feet in size and hung on steel cables with four wheels. Another cable would run through the center between the others at about waist high. That cable was the one you would grab onto and pull yourself across with.

We sent the mules around with the local guide and took turns in the rickety horizontal contraption hoping it could handle its live cargo that was built in the USA. It did, and we soon made it to the second village. Every village I ever entered in the jungle was special. The people were always glad to see you and appreciated you being there to help. Because safe clean drinking water was not available to us, the women in the village would collect water from the closest source and boil it for us. This would sanitize it but didn't do much for the taste. Some of the guys even nicknamed this beverage smoke water for its distinctive flavor. But being in that Amazon heat, we needed to drink as much as possible.

As we would work, the ladies of the village would come to the job site periodically and hand us fresh mango and a turtle shell full of water. We'd stop and take the offering given to us and thank them for taking good care of us. Most of the time, the water was still warm having recently come off the fire. But once in a while, you'd be handed a shell of cool water that you knew came right out of a stream somewhere. At that point, it was too late to do anything about it but smile at your hostess, who didn't get the memo to boil it, and thank them. They were only trying to be a blessing. They were so appreciative to have us there. I would remind the Lord of that after every cool drink I consumed. God protected us big time in this area.

In the middle of the day while we were working on this second church, the normal sounds were interrupted with a huge "Kapow!" coming from out in the surrounding jungle. It echoed throughout the foothills. It was definitely a gunshot, but nobody out here had guns, only machetes. About twenty minutes later, a man arrived carrying a recently shot rodent of about eight to ten pounds. He also had a homemade pistol constructed from a pipe and rebar...impressive.

He was proud of his recent kill as he should have been and proceeded to prepare it for us for dinner that night. As unappetizing as that sounds, all the different types of jungle rats I've eaten in the Amazon have always been pretty good and are a perfect entrée to a heaping side of ever-present yuca.

After finishing the second church, we hiked farther into the third village to continue our work. We were always careful to arrive before sundown. You never wanted to get caught out there on the path in the dark. It's just not a wise move. As we prepped the site on the third project, there was a palm tree that was going to be too close to the structure and needed to come out. Most palms are very soft, and this one was chopped down quickly and removed. To my surprise, for the next several meals, there were platters of fresh palm heart on the table...next to the yuca of course. I've never eaten a tree that I helped cut down before, and it was delicious.

Soon we were off again, deeper still into the jungle to the fourth village. It was more of the same—beautiful smiles from the villagers, turtle shells of smoke water, and copious amounts of yuca. To our astonishment, the Lord gave us the safety and health to complete all four churches within our time schedule. We were happy, and so were the mules. All we had to do now was to retrace our steps and hike a few days to get back to the outpost.

We had to push it one of these days to get to the village where we planned to spend that night. As the sun was going down, it was soon apparent that we weren't going to make it there before dark. That wasn't good. I call this time of night "feeding time." For several hours, we struggled on those unfamiliar jungle paths in that blackness. We used our flashlights sparingly to conserve the batteries. We soon made it up a rise and found our desired village. Praise the Lord we didn't lose anyone or break anyone.

As we finally made it back to the outpost and loaded ourselves into the back of the pickup for the scenic ride back to civilization, Doc shared with us. He told us how much he enjoyed doing this mission with us. These were four villages with established congregations that were routinely being checked on, but he personally hadn't been able to get to them in about twenty years. They had always been in his heart, but what a joy to see them and work with them after so many years. Then he started handing each of us a couple of pills and said, "Here, take these. If you guys didn't get worms on this trip, you'll never get them." That was comforting. I guess consuming twenty pounds of yuca in a week and a half doesn't counteract that deal.

What Doc said about those villages really hit home to me. The villages we usually worked in were always on a main river or at least a good-sized one that was somewhat accessible. These weren't. The only way to really reach them was to hike in through the "back door" of the jungle. They were so remote that even Doc, who had lived forty years in the Amazon, hadn't made it to them in twenty.

Yet God was out there and had always been there, loving and nourishing His people, and they accepted us as their brothers when we showed up. Just how big is the God we serve? One day we will sit together with our Aguaruna family in heaven at the marriage supper of the Lamb and share a meal together. If I see a platter of yuca, I'll know who to pass it to.

> Where can I go from Your Spirit? Or where can I flee from Your presence? If I ascend into heaven, You are there; if I make my bed in hell,

behold, You are there. If I take the wings of the morning, and dwell in the uttermost parts of the sea, even there Your hand shall lead me, and Your right hand shall hold me.
—Psalm 139:7–10

CHAPTER 32

ENLIGHTEN ME

For centuries, the land of Nepal has been sought out by the world as one of the centers of spirituality. This became even more evident in the last century as people flocked there as they turned to Eastern religions in an attempt to find some form of enlightenment. It is this Nepal that is part of the South Asia field that Dave and I frequented in establishing the Work & Witness program. We also had the privilege to lead a number of teams there.

One of the main purposes of taking these teams to Nepal was to erect Child Development Centers and local churches. As beautiful as the country is with the Himalayas rising into the sky, it is the people who are even more beautiful. Their gentle spirits and broad smiles would always brighten your day. That's why one encounter was rather puzzling as we worked on a job site in the southern town of Bardaghat.

We had just finished a project in the east in a town called Itahari. We always had local help in our construction efforts, and Itahari and Bardaghat were no different. Typically several local men and women were on site during the workday laboring side by side with their brothers and sisters from America. For the most part, they were always cordial and fun-loving as we got to know each other. But there was one particular woman on the Bardaghat site who never smiled or laughed with the others. We'll call her Rachel.[5]

Rachel was an attractive young woman who was probably in her early to midtwenties. She stood out because she always wore a bright red top on the job site. But Rachel was beginning to stand out even more because of her melancholy demeanor. After a few days, someone asked one of the local workers if Rachel was OK, or if something was going on in her life. She had the look of carrying a heavy load. What we were told shocked us all.

Just a few days before we arrived, Rachel had let her toddler outside to play for a while. While her little child was enjoying himself, he was bitten by a cobra and passed away almost instantly. Rachel was still in shock over it. I couldn't believe she was even there with us, but she showed up every day.

There just happened to be a woman on our team who had suffered the loss of her own child in a car accident many years before. None of us knew this. Being a few years older than Rachel, the woman was able to sit down with her and, through an interpreter, minister to Rachel about how God pulled her through such a tragedy. The countenance of this mourning mother changed, and I even saw Rachel smile a few times after this encounter. I thought about how awesome it was that God met the needs of one of His suffering daughters with another one from halfway around the world at just the right time. Our times in Nepal were always exciting and fruitful. Whether it was taking JESUS Film equipment through customs or watching the sun come up over the distant peak of Mount Everest

---

[5] Rachel—name changed to protect her.

early one morning. The leaders we worked with were using a variety of methods to reach their people with the Gospel. JESUS Film equipment wasn't the only thing we took into Nepal. Other ministry tools were taken in as well.

One of these tools was soccer balls that were made in the colors that depicted the Gospel story. Patches of black, red, white, gold, and green covered these soccer balls better known as Evangeballs. With the world's passion for soccer, these balls are very popular among young people and not-so-young people alike. I had the honor to stand before a good-sized group of young people with one of these balls in my hand and share with them how our sin (black) has separated us from God. But Jesus came and shed His blood (red) to eliminate that separation if we accept Him. When we put our trust in Jesus, He takes our sins away and purifies us (white). Because of that, we are promised to go to heaven (gold) when we die and have eternal life (green) with God there. This tool is effective in any language and was that day too as I led them in prayer. These soccer balls are popular in many places around the globe.

Christians in this part of the world are an extreme minority and aren't always treated with the best intentions. This became apparent during one church service we attended. A good-sized rock hit the roof in the middle of the service while I was speaking. It had been launched from a temple of another religion that stood on a bluff overlooking this church. We were all just glad it didn't come through the roof. I was beginning to develop a complex about my preaching.

Katmandu is home of two of the most famous temples in the world. In fact, they're deemed to be sacred. One is Buddhist, and the other is Hindu. In a society that is desperately looking for spiritual answers to their broken lives, people from around the world still flock to these sites today. We had a chance to check them out in our travels to Nepal. This is what I experienced at one of them.

As we approached the temple, we walked down the main road that led to the entrance of the grounds. Both sides of the street were flooded with shops and open-air tables loaded with statues and idols of Hindu gods and temple souvenirs. As I got closer, I could feel a spiritual oppression get thicker. Occasionally I would pass a so-called holy man with long unkempt hair and a long beard to match.

These guys would be painted up in ritual colors on their skin, which was plentiful because they were practically naked. This "getup" and their mannerisms made them look otherworldly.

Once we got into the temple grounds, I noticed a low-flowing river running through the center of everything. There was a large platform on one side of this river. We happened to be there as a Hindu funeral was getting ready to take place on this platform. We watched from the opposite side of the river as the deceased was laid out on a waist-high table-like structure and was prepared with piles of wood that would soon be lit to consume the body.

Once the body is burned, the attendants just dump the remains into the river in front of the platform. I looked into the river to see piles of charred remains from these types of rituals that had recently taken place. Someone had obviously shoveled them further down this section of the river to make room for the new piles that would soon take their place.

Flies and stench were everywhere, and an overwhelming sense of hopelessness could easily consume you if you let it. I thought, *Why in the world would people come to a place like this for spiritual enlightenment?* There was nothing here but the spirit of death and despair. It was so thick, you could feel it. I thought of what Rachel had just gone through. What sort of hope would she have if she had to come to a place like this for spiritual guidance?

Yet there are still millions of Rachels caught in this cycle who haven't heard about or had the chance to meet the living God. A Savior Who loves and cares for us so much that He would even send someone halfway around the world to minister to one of His hurting daughters. That's the God of life and hope. I always left Nepal thinking, *We need to do more.*

> I call heaven and earth as witnesses today against you, that I have set before you life and death, blessing and cursing; therefore choose life, that both you and your descendants may live;

that you may love the Lord your God, that you may obey His voice, and that you may cling to Him, for He is your life and the length of your days.

—Deuteronomy 30:19–20A

THE STORY CONTINUES

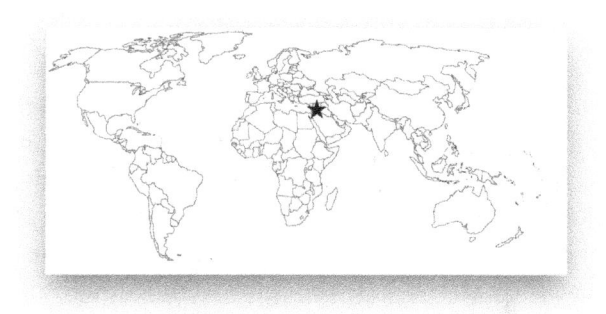

I suppose this is where writers like to put a conclusion or epilogue to their books. I don't see it that way. What I've shared with you in the previous pages is a glimpse into just some of the activities that God is still doing. My guess is that He will continue to do similar things and brand-new ones until He says that it's time for a conclusion. I'm hoping that He still trusts me enough to continue to work with Him in His new adventures around the world. So far He has, as He is still helping me today to get equipment and ministry tools into places that need it.

I posed a question to you way back in the introduction. Is God still active today in His pursuit to bring humanity into a personal relationship with Him, or is He just the God on the pages of a two-thousand-year-old book? All of us make that decision on our own. I think you know what my answer is. Hopefully I have been able, in some way, to help you make your decision too.

I had been invited to go help out a team that was going to do a project in Jordan. But before we went to Jordan, they had decided to spend a few days in Israel and check out the sites there. I had never expected to go to the Holy Land, but it was a nice surprise when I found out. We saw several major biblical areas while we were there, but there was one that really hit home with me.

We had toured the old city of Jerusalem one day and saw all the big stuff—the church of the Holy Sepulchre, the Via Dolorosa, the Western Wall, as well as some others including the house of Caiaphas the High Priest. Then the next day, we were able to go over to the Mount of Olives. We had a chance to split up by ourselves and have some solitude as we walked among the olive trees on the side of that hill.

I spent some time praying and thinking about where I was. This was where Jesus and the twelve spent a lot of time together. They may have even slept out here some nights. It's also the place Jesus said goodbye in the physical to His followers as He ascended off the top of the hill. He has promised to return to the same place when He comes back to earth. These thoughts went through my mind as I slowly made my way down through the olive trees.

I couldn't help but look across the Kidron Valley to the walled city of Jerusalem that was laid out before me. It was the classic picture you always see of Jerusalem with the Dome of the Rock sitting on top of the Temple Mount, but this day it wasn't a picture—it was real life.

As I got to the bottom of the Mount of Olives, I was entering the Garden of Gethsemane. It was right into the area where Jesus went with the elven after the Last Supper. I looked at the ancient olive trees that are still standing there and the olive press that is present. Then I lifted my eyes back across the Kidron Valley and toward the city of Jerusalem again...and then it hit me.

I could see where I had been the day before. I could see where Judas and the temple guard would have left with torches lit to come arrest Jesus. I could see what Jesus saw. That means Jesus would have seen them coming. A band of men with torches lit at night walking out of an unelectrified city down through the Kidron Valley and across to the Garden would definitely stand out. It would have taken several minutes to make this hike. It dawned on me that Jesus stayed right there watching them.

About two miles behind the Mount of Olives was the town of Bethany. Jesus had good friends and contacts in that town like Lazarus, Martha, and Mary. How easy it would have been to go there as soon as He saw the torches coming. But He stayed right there and waited. Of course, being Jesus, He could have just disappeared or called just one angel to wipe out the mob instantly. He chose not to. He stayed right there as the torches got closer and closer.

I had never thought about it before until this moment of God revealing it to me. Jesus saw them the whole way, knowing what they were coming to do to Him. His first act of giving up Himself for me, or us, on His way to the cross was done right where I was standing. I was overwhelmed just thinking about it.

Maybe you never really thought about it before. We always hear about Jesus dying on the cross and rising from the dead, but we don't think about the series of conscious decisions of self-sacrifice that Jesus made to get to that point. That's the kind of God we have and wants to partner with us in His work to reach others. It's incredible.

If you know about Jesus but don't really know Him in a personal way, you probably aren't sure what I'm talking about. Jesus said there is only one way to the Father (or heaven), and that is through Jesus Himself. Those are His words, not mine. I think God was trying to make it simple for us and not create a bunch of confusion.

If you're not sure about your relationship with Jesus, it's very easy to get it right. According to the Bible, all you have to do is acknowledge that you are separated from God by your sins and change your mind about the direction that your life has been going. Then trust that Jesus is the Son of God like He claimed to be and that He came to die for your sins that you just acknowledged. Then ask God to forgive you of those sins, and believe that Jesus rose again from the dead to defeat death for you. And invite Jesus to come live in your heart.

That prayer should sound like this: "Lord, I know I'm a sinner and separated from You. I believe Jesus is the Son of God and died on the cross to save me and rose from the dead on the third day. Forgive me of my sins. I repent and confess Jesus as my Lord and Savior. I surrender to Him and invite Him into my heart." If you pray that simple prayer with your mouth to God and believe it with your heart, He has promised to forgive you and start a brand-new relationship with you. I encourage you to pray that prayer. I can tell you there is no ride in life like a personal relationship with the Creator of the universe.

You may already be in a relationship with Jesus, but you feel like you can't figure out what your purpose in life really is. Week after week, month after month, or maybe even year after year keep clicking by, and the busyness of life keeps you from thinking about it very much until you get that rare quiet time. You are not alone. I believe it is plaguing many Christians in today's age.

If you are in this boat, make it known to God. He likes to listen to us. But then keep your eyes and heart alert for open doors that He lays before you. Don't worry. He's not going to ask everyone to try to start a church or bypass customs in Timbuktu. But He might want you to say "Yes" to leading that Bible study or jumping into a ministry that you've always wondered about or just talking to that coworker about the Lord who you've been too nervous to address.

At some point, we have to step out and join Him in His adventure. We have to make conscious decisions of faith into the unknown the way Jesus made them when He knew what was coming in the garden. I know from experience, when we step out into the unknown, God will always be there with us. Maybe not always the way we think He might be there, but He will be there. He promised He would be. Be flexible in your faith, and be willing to be used by Him and with Him. When we do this, our tomorrow will truly be beautiful.

> For You, Lord, are good, and ready to forgive, And abundant in mercy to all those who call upon You.
> —Psalm 86:5

The will of God is always a bigger thing than we bargain for, but we must believe that whatever it involves, it is good, acceptable and perfect.

—Jim Elliot

For more information on the ministries that have been mentioned in this book:

    Compassion575: compassion575.com
    Work & Witness: nazarene.org/workandwitness
    JESUS Film Harvest Partners: jfhp.org
    Nazarene Compassionate Ministries: ncm.org
    Cru (Campus Crusade for Christ): cru.org

    Email with any comments or questions:

    tomorrowisbeautifulbook@gmail.com
    (I'll do my best to get back to you.)

Printed in the USA
CPSIA information can be obtained
at www.ICGtesting.com
CBHW020815251124
17828CB00001B/3